HSP Science

Assessment Guide

Grade 3

Harcourt
SCHOOL PUBLISHERS

Visit *The Learning Site!*
www.harcourtschool.com

Copyright © by Harcourt, Inc.

All rights reserved. No part of this publication may be reproduced or transmitted in any form or by any means, electronic or mechanical, including photocopy, recording, or any information storage and retrieval system, without permission in writing from the publisher.

Permission is hereby granted to individuals using the corresponding student's textbook or kit as the major vehicle for regular classroom instruction to photocopy Copying Masters from this publication in classroom quantities for instructional use and not for resale. Requests for information on other matters regarding duplication of this work should be addressed to School Permissions and Copyrights, Harcourt, Inc., 6277 Sea Harbor Drive, Orlando, Florida 32887-6777. Fax: 407-345-2418.

HARCOURT and the Harcourt Logo are trademarks of Harcourt, Inc., registered in the United States of America and/or other jurisdictions.

Printed in the United States of America

ISBN – 13: 978-0-15-361045-5

ISBN – 10: 0-15-361045-X

1 2 3 4 5 6 7 8 9 10 054 16 15 14 13 12 11 10 09 08 07

If you have received these materials as examination copies free of charge, Harcourt School Publishers retains title to the materials and they may not be resold. Resale of examination copies is strictly prohibited and is illegal.

Possession of this publication in print format does not entitle users to convert this publication, or any portion of it, into electronic format.

Contents

Overview . . . . AGv
Assessment Components . . . . AGv
Formal Assessment . . . . AGviii
Test-Taking Tips . . . . AGix
Performance Assessment . . . . AGx
Scoring a Performance Task . . . . AGxii
Classroom Observation . . . . AGxiii
Observation Checklist . . . . AGxv
Using Student Self-Assessment . . . . AGxvi
Self-Assessment—Read and Learn . . . . AGxvii
Experiment/Project Evaluation Checklist . . . . AGxviii
Experiment/Project Summary Sheet . . . . AGxix
Portfolio Assessment . . . . AGxx
Science Experiences Record . . . . AGxxii
Guide to My Science Portfolio . . . . AGxxiii
Portfolio Evaluation Checklist . . . . AGxxiv

Introduction—Getting Ready for Science . . . . AGxxv

Unit A: Living Things in Our World
Chapter 1—Types of Living Things AG1
Performance Task AG5
Chapter 2—Types of Plants AG7
Performance Task AG11
Chapter 3—Types of Animals AG13
Performance Task AG17
Unit A Assessment AG19

Unit B: Living Things Interact
Chapter 4—Where Living Things Are Found AG25
Performance Task AG29
Chapter 5—Living Things Depend on One Another . . AG31
Performance Task AG35
Unit B Assessment AG37

Unit C: Earth's Land
Chapter 6—Minerals and Rocks. AG43
Performance Task AG47
Chapter 7—Forces That Shape the Land AG49
Performance Task AG53
Chapter 8—Conserving Resources. AG55
Performance Task AG59
Unit C Assessment AG61

Unit D: Weather and Space
Chapter 9—The Water Cycle AG67
Performance Task AG71
Chapter 10—Earth's Place in the Solar System . AG73
Performance Task AG77
Unit D Assessment AG79

Unit E: Investigating Matter and Energy
Chapter 11—Properties of Matter AG85
Performance Task AG89
Chapter 12—Energy AG91
Performance Task AG95
Chapter 13—Electricity and Magnets. AG97
Performance Task AG101
Chapter 14—Heat, Light, and Sound AG103
Performance Task AG107
Unit E Assessment AG109

Unit F: Exploring Forces and Motion
Chapter 15—Forces and Motion AG115
Performance Task AG119
Chapter 16—Work and Machines. AG121
Performance Task AG125
Unit F Assessment AG127

Answer Key AG133–AG158

Overview

In *HSP Science*, the assessment program, like the instruction, is student-oriented. By allowing all learners to show what they know and can do, the program provides you with ongoing information about each student's understanding of science. Equally important, the assessment program offers ample opportunity for students to evaluate their own growth.

The assessment program in *HSP Science* offers the assessment options shown in the chart below. The various options reveal the multidimensional aspect of the program.

Assessment Options

Formal Assessment	Ongoing Assessment	Performance Assessment
• Chapter Review and Test Preparation SE • Chapter Test AG • Unit Test AG	• Assess Prior Knowledge—Chapter Opener TE • Daily Inquiry Transparencies • Teacher Edition questions throughout • Focus Skill questions throughout SE • Differentiated Instruction throughout TE • Lesson Review SE • Observation Checklist AG	• Long-Option AG • Short-Option TE
Standardized Test Preparation • Lesson Review SE		**Student Self-Assessment** • Investigate Self-Assessment Lab Manual • Self-Assessment AG
Online Assessment • Online chapter and unit tests with automatic scoring • Item bank from which to build tests		**Portfolio Assessment** • Using Portfolio Assessment AG • Suggested work samples TE

(Key: SE = Student Edition; TE = Teacher Edition; AG = Assessment Guide)

Assessment Components

Formal Assessment

To help you reinforce and assess mastery of chapter objectives, *HSP Science* includes both reviews and tests. You will find the Chapter Review and Test Preparation in the student book and the Chapter Test and Unit Test in this **Assessment Guide.** Answers to all assessments, including sample responses to constructed-response items, are provided.

Grade 3   Assessment Guide

Standardized Test Preparation
Large-scale assessment of science literacy has been mandated by the *No Child Left Behind Act (NCLB)*, the 2001 reauthorization of the Elementary and Secondary Education Act. To help prepare students for district- or state-mandated assessments, *HSP Science* includes items that reflect the format of standardized tests. These items can be found in each Lesson Review and Chapter Review and Test Prep in the **Student Edition.**

Online Assessment
The ability to deliver tests online provides the teacher with increased flexibility in managing classroom assessment. The Chapter Tests and Unit Tests that appear in this **Assessment Guide** can be delivered online. In addition, *Online Assessment* allows you to assemble custom tests from a bank of multiple-choice, short-response, and extended-response items. Multiple-choice items are scored automatically, and a user-friendly interface allows teachers to enter scores for short- and extended-response items. You can also build tests according to state standards. For more information, visit **www.hspscience.com.**

Ongoing Assessment
HSP Science supports ongoing assessment in several ways. Within each lesson in the **Student Edition**, there is a Focus Skill question at the end of each section to help you assess students' immediate recall of information. At the end of each lesson is a Lesson Review to help you evaluate how well students grasped the concepts taught.

The **Teacher Edition** offers a number of informal assessment tools. By using the Assess Prior Knowledge that accompanies each chapter opener, you can gauge students' foundational knowledge. Daily Inquiry Transparencies are designed to reinforce and evaluate students' use of inquiry skills. Questions that address a variety of dimensions—including critical thinking skills, inquiry skills, and use of reading strategies—are strategically placed throughout each lesson. Additional material for reviewing the lesson is provided in **Reading Support and Homework.** Located in this **Assessment Guide** is yet another tool, the Observation Checklist (p. AGxv), on which you can record noteworthy classroom observations.

Performance Assessment
Performance tasks provide evidence of students' ability to use science inquiry skills and critical thinking skills to complete an authentic task. A brief performance task is included as part of the information in the **Teacher Edition** that accompanies each chapter review. A more comprehensive performance task follows each Chapter Test in this **Assessment Guide.** Each includes teacher directions and a scoring rubric. Also in this booklet, you will find the Experiment/Project Evaluation Checklist (p. AGxviii) for evaluating unit inquiries and projects.

Student Self-Assessment

Students should be challenged to reflect on their work and to monitor and control their own learning. Various checklists are provided for this purpose. An Investigate Self-Assessment accompanies each Investigate in the **Lab Manual** in Grades 3–6. This simple checklist allows students to evaluate their performance, using criteria specific to each activity. Two checklists are located in this **Assessment Guide.** One is the Self-Assessment—Read and Learn (p. AGxvii), which helps students reflect on instruction in a particular lesson or chapter. The other is the Experiment/Project Summary Sheet (p. AGxix), on which students describe and evaluate their own science projects and experiments.

Portfolio Assessment

In *HSP Science*, students may create their own portfolios. The portfolio contains self-selected work samples that the student feels represent increased science literacy. The portfolio may also contain a few required or teacher-selected papers. Support materials are included in this **Assessment Guide** (pp. AGxx–AGxxiv) to assist you and your students in developing portfolios.

Formal Assessment

Formal assessment is an essential part of any comprehensive assessment program because it provides an objective measure of student achievement. This traditional form of assessment typically consists of reviews and tests that assess how well students understand, communicate, and apply what they have learned.

Formal Assessment in *HSP Science*

Formal assessment in *HSP Science* includes the following tools: Chapter Review and Test Preparation in the **Student Edition** and Chapter and Unit Assessments in this **Assessment Guide**. The purpose of the review is to assess and reinforce not only chapter concepts and inquiry skills but also students' test-taking skills. The purpose of the Chapter and Unit Assessments is, as with other formal assessments, to provide an objective measure of student performance. Answers to chapter reviews, including sample responses to constructed-response items, are located in the **Teacher Edition**, while answers to chapter and unit tests are located in the Answer Key in this booklet.

The chapter and unit tests that appear in this **Assessment Guide** may be delivered electronically by using *Online Assessment*. For more information, visit **www.hspscience.com**.

Types of Review and Test Items

Students can be overwhelmed by the amount of information on a test and uneasy about how to answer different types of test questions. The Chapter Review and Test Preparation is designed to help familiarize students with the various item formats they may encounter: *multiple-choice items* (with a question stem; graph, table, map, diagram, model, or picture; or using qualifiers such as *not*, *least*, and so on), *constructed-response items* (which, depending on grade level, require the student to write a short or an extended answer), and *context-dependent sets*, in which the student is asked to respond to related items.

Test-Taking Tips

Understandably, students often experience test-related anxiety. Teaching students to apply a number of general test-taking strategies may bolster their confidence and result in improved student performance on formal assessment. As students take a test, they should

- scan the entire test first before answering any questions.
- read the directions slowly and carefully before beginning a section.
- begin with the easiest questions or most familiar material.
- read the question and all answer options before selecting an answer.
- watch out for key words such as *not*, *least*, *best*, *most,* and so on.
- carefully analyze graphs, tables, diagrams, and pictures that accompany items.
- double-check answers to catch and correct errors.
- erase all mistakes completely and write corrections neatly.

Test Preparation

Students perform better on formal assessments when they are well prepared for the testing situation. Here are some things you can do before a test to help your students do their best work.

- Explain the nature of the test to students.
- Suggest that they review the questions at the end of the lessons and the chapter.
- Remind students to get a good night's sleep before the test.
- Discuss why they should eat a balanced meal beforehand.
- Encourage students to relax while they take the test.

Performance Assessment

Teachers today have come to realize that the multiple-choice format of traditional tests, while useful and efficient, cannot provide a complete picture of students' growth in science. Standardized multiple-choice tests cannot fully reveal how students *think and do things*—an essential aspect of science literacy. Performance assessment can provide this missing information and help balance your assessment program. Well-constructed performance assessments provide a window through which teachers may view students' thought processes.

An important feature of performance assessment is that it involves a hands-on activity in which students solve a situational problem. Students often find performance assessment more enjoyable than traditional paper-and-pencil tests. Another advantage is that it models good instruction: students are assessed as they learn and learn as they are assessed.

Performance Assessment in *HSP Science*

Performance tasks can be found in two locations in *HSP Science*. In the **Teacher Edition**, a brief performance task is part of the information that accompanies each chapter review. In this **Assessment Guide**, a more comprehensive task follows each chapter test. Both types of performance tasks will provide insights into students' ability to apply key science inquiry skills and concepts taught in the chapter. You may use the Experiment/Project Evaluation Checklist (p. AGxviii) to evaluate student performance on these tasks.

Administering Performance Tasks

Unlike traditional assessment tools, performance assessment does not provide standardized directions for its administration or impose specific time limits on students, although a suggested time frame is offered as a guideline. The suggestions that follow may help you define your role in this assessment.

- *Be prepared.*
  A few days before students begin the task, read the Teacher's Directions and gather the materials needed.

- *Be clear.*
  Explain the directions for the task; rephrase them as needed. Also, explain how students' performance will be evaluated. Show students the rubric you plan to use, and explain the performance indicators in language your students understand.

- *Be encouraging.*
  Your role in administering the assessments should be that of a coach—motivating, guiding, and encouraging students to produce their best work.

- *Be supportive.*
  You may assist students who need help. The amount of assistance needed will depend on the needs and abilities of individual students.

- *Be flexible.*
  Not all students need to proceed through the performance task at the same rate and in the same manner. Allow students adequate time to do their best work.

- *Involve students in evaluation.*
  Invite students to join you as partners in the evaluation process, particularly in development or modification of the rubric.

Rubrics for Assessing Performance

A well-written rubric can help you score students' work accurately and fairly. Moreover, before students begin a task, it gives them a better idea of what qualities their work should exhibit.

Each performance task in the program has its own rubric. The rubric lists performance indicators, which are brief statements of what to look for in assessing the skills and understandings that the task addresses. A sample rubric for a task in this **Assessment Guide** follows.

Scoring Rubric

Performance Indicators

_____ Assembles the kite successfully.

_____ Carries out the experiment daily.

_____ Records results accurately.

_____ Makes an accurate chart and uses it to report the strength of wind observed each day.

Observations and Rubric Score

| 3 | 2 | 1 | 0 |

Scoring a Performance Task

The scoring system used for performance tasks in this **Assessment Guide** is a 4-point scale that is compatible with those used by many state assessment programs. You may wish to modify the rubrics as a 3- or 5-point scale. To determine a student's score on a performance task, review the indicators checked on the rubric and then select the score that best represents the student's overall performance on the task.

4-Point Scale			
Excellent Achievement	Adequate Achievement	Limited Achievement	Little or No Achievement
3	2	1	0

How to Convert a Rubric Score into a Grade

If, for grading purposes, you want to record a letter or numerical grade rather than a holistic score for the student's performance on a task, you can use the following conversion table:

Holistic Score	Letter Grade	Numerical Grade
3	A	90–100
2	B	80–89
1	C	70–79
0	D–F	69 or below

Developing Your Own Rubric

From time to time, you may want to either develop your own rubric or work together with your students to create one. Research has shown that significantly improved performance can result from student participation in the construction of rubrics.

Developing a rubric for a performance task involves three basic steps: (1) Identify the inquiry skills that are taught in the chapter and that students must perform to complete the task successfully, and identify what understanding of content is also required. (2) Determine which skills and understandings are involved in each step. (3) Decide what you will look for to confirm that the student has acquired each skill and understanding you identified.

Assessment Guide

Classroom Observation

"Kid watching" is a natural part of teaching and an important part of evaluation. The purpose of classroom observation in assessment is to gather and record information that can lead to improved instruction. In this booklet, you will find an Observation Checklist (p. AGxv) on which you can record noteworthy observations of students' ability to use science inquiry skills.

Using the Observation Checklist

- ***Identify the skills you will observe.***
  Find out which inquiry skills are introduced and reinforced in the chapter.

- ***Focus on only a few students at a time.***
  You will find this more effective than trying to observe the entire class at once.

- ***Look for a pattern.***
  It is important to observe a student's strengths and weaknesses over a period of time to determine whether a pattern exists.

- ***Plan how and when to record observations.***
  Decide whether to

  —record observations immediately on the checklist as you move about the room or

  —make jottings or mental notes of observations and record them later.

- ***Don't agonize over the ratings.***
  Students who stand out as particularly strong will clearly merit a rating of *3* ("Outstanding"). Others may clearly earn a rating of *1* ("Needs Improvement"). This doesn't mean, however, that a *2* ("Satisfactory") is automatically the appropriate rating for the rest of the class. For example, you may not have had sufficient opportunity to observe a student demonstrate certain skills. The checklist cells for these skills should remain blank under the student's name until you have observed him or her perform the skills.

- ***Review your checklist periodically, and ask yourself questions such as:***

  What are the student's strongest/weakest attributes?

  In what ways has the student shown growth?

  In what areas does the class as a whole show strength/weakness?

  What kinds of activities would encourage growth?

  Do I need to allot more time to classroom observation?

- **Use the data you collect.**
  Refer to your classroom observation checklists when you plan lessons, form groups, assign grades, and confer with students and family members.

Date _____

Observation Checklist

Rating Scale	
3 Outstanding	1 Needs Improvement
2 Satisfactory	☐ Not Enough Opportunity to Observe

Names of Students

Inquiry Skills											
Observe											
Compare											
Classify/Order											
Gather, Record, Display, or Interpret Data											
Use Numbers											
Communicate											
Plan and Conduct Simple Investigations											
Measure											
Predict											
Infer											
Draw Conclusions											
Use Time/Space Relationships											
Hypothesize											
Formulate or Use Models											
Identify and Control Variables											
Experiment											

Grade 3

Using Student Self-Assessment

Researchers have evidence that self-evaluation and the reflection it involves can have positive effects on students' learning. To achieve these effects, students must be challenged to reflect on their work and to monitor, analyze, and control their own learning—beginning in the earliest grades.

Frequent opportunities for students to evaluate their performance build the skills and confidence they need for effective self-assessment. A trusting relationship between the student and the teacher is also essential. Students must be assured that honest responses can have only a positive effect on the teacher's view of them and that they will not be used to determine grades.

Student Self-Assessment in *HSP Science*

The assessment program offers three self-assessment measures. In Grades 3–6, an Investigate Self-Assessment is part of each Investigate in the **Lab Manual.** This simple checklist allows students to evaluate their performance, using criteria that are specific to each activity. Two checklists are found in this **Assessment Guide.** One is Self-Assessment—Read and Learn: a form that leads students to reflect on and evaluate what they learned from reading at the lesson or chapter level. The second is the Experiment/Project Summary Sheet—a form that helps students describe and evaluate their unit inquiries and projects.

Using Self-Assessment Forms

- *Explain the directions.*
  Discuss the forms and how to complete them.

- *Encourage honest responses.*
  Be sure to tell students that there are no "right" responses to the items.

- *Model the process.*
  One way to foster candid responses is to model the process yourself, including at least one response that is not positive. Discuss reasons for your responses.

- *Be open to variations in students' responses.*
  Negative responses should not be viewed as indicating weaknesses. Rather, they confirm that you did a good job of communicating the importance of honesty in self-assessment.

- *Discuss responses with students.*
  You may wish to clarify students' responses in conferences with them and in family conferences. Invite both students and family members to help you plan activities for school and home that will motivate and support students' growth in science.

Name _____
Date _____
Lesson or Chapter _____

**Self-Assessment—
Read and Learn**

My Thoughts Exactly!

Decide whether you agree or disagree with each statement below. Circle the word that tells what you think. If you are not sure, circle the question mark.

1. The pictures and captions in the book helped me understand what I was reading.	**Agree** ?	**Disagree**
2. When I didn't understand, I asked questions.	**Agree** ?	**Disagree**
3. I learned a lot from class discussions.	**Agree** ?	**Disagree**
4. I used the (Focus Skill) questions and the review questions to test my understanding.	**Agree** ?	**Disagree**
5. I understand the new science terms.	**Agree** ?	**Disagree**
6. I have a good understanding of the topic.	**Agree** ?	**Disagree**
7. I think I am doing well in science.	**Agree** ?	**Disagree**

Think about what you learned. Then complete each sentence.

8. Three things I learned about the topic are _____
_____
_____.

9. I learned these new science terms: _____
_____
_____

Grade 3 Assessment Guide **AG xvii**

Experiment/Project Evaluation Checklist

Name _____

Date _____

Experiment/Project Evaluation

Aspects of Science Literacy	Evidence of Growth
1. **Understands science concepts** *(Animals, Plants; Earth's Land, Air, Water; Space; Weather; Matter, Motion, Energy)*	
2. **Uses inquiry skills** *(observes, compares, classifies, gathers/ interprets data, communicates, measures, experiments, infers, predicts, draws conclusions)*	
3. **Thinks critically** *(analyzes, synthesizes, evaluates, applies ideas effectively, solves problems)*	
4. **Displays traits/attitudes of a scientist** *(is curious, questioning, persistent, precise, creative, enthusiastic; uses science materials carefully; is concerned for environment)*	

Summary Evaluation/Teacher Comments: _____

_____

_____

_____

_____

Name _____

Date _____

Experiment/Project Summary Sheet

You can tell about your science project or experiment by completing the following sentences.

My Experiment/Project

1. My experiment/project was about _____
_____
_____

2. I worked on this experiment/project with _____
_____
_____

3. I gathered information from these sources: _____
_____
_____

4. The most important thing I learned from doing this experiment/project is _____
_____
_____

5. I think I did a (an) _____ job on my experiment/project because
_____
_____

6. I'd also like to tell you _____
_____
_____
_____

Grade 3　　　　　　　　　　　　　　　　　Assessment Guide　**AG xix**

Portfolio Assessment

A portfolio is a showcase for student work, a place where many types of assignments, projects, reports, and writings can be collected. The work samples in the collection provide "snapshots" of the student's efforts over time, and taken together they reveal the student's growth, attitudes, and understanding better than any other type of assessment. However, portfolios are not ends in themselves. Their value comes from creating them, discussing them, and using them to improve learning.

The purpose of using portfolios in science is threefold:

- *To give the student a voice in the assessment process.*
- *To foster reflection, self-monitoring, and self-evaluation.*
- *To provide a comprehensive picture of a student's progress.*

Portfolio Assessment in *HSP Science*

In *HSP Science*, students may assemble portfolio collections of their work. The collection may include a few required papers, such as chapter tests, performance tasks, and Experiment/Project Evaluation forms.

From time to time, consider including other measures (Science Experiences Record, Experiment/Project Summary Sheet, and Self-Assessment—Read and Learn). The Science Experiences Record, for example, can reveal insights about student interests, ideas, and out-of-school experiences (museum visits, nature walks, outside readings, and so on) that otherwise you might not know about. Materials to help you and your students build portfolios and use them for evaluation are included in the pages that follow.

Using Portfolio Assessment

- ***Explain the portfolio and its use.***
  Describe how people in many fields use portfolios to present samples of their work when they are applying for a job. Tell students that they can create their own portfolio to show what they have learned, what skills they have acquired, and how they think they are doing in science.

- ***Decide what standard pieces should be included.***
  Encourage students to identify a few standard, or "required," work samples that they will include in their portfolios, and discuss reasons for including them. The Student Task sheets for the performance assessments in this **Assessment Guide**, for example, might be a standard sample in the portfolios because they show students' ability to use inquiry skills and critical thinking skills. Together with your class, decide on the required work samples that everyone's portfolio will include.

- ***Discuss student-selected work samples.***
  Point out that the best work to select is not necessarily the longest or the neatest. Rather, it is work the student believes will best demonstrate his or her growth in science understanding and skills.

- ***Establish a basic plan.***
  Decide about how many work samples will be included in the portfolio and when they should be selected. Ask students to list on the Guide to My Science Portfolio (p. AGxxiii) each sample they select and to explain why they selected it.

- ***Tell students how you will evaluate their portfolios.***
  Use a blank Portfolio Evaluation sheet to explain how you will evaluate the contents of a portfolio.

- ***Use the portfolio.***
  Use the portfolio as a handy reference tool in determining students' science grades and in holding conferences with them and family members. You may wish to send the portfolio home for family members to review.

Science Experiences Record

Name _____

Date _____

My Science Experiences

Date	What I Did	What I Thought or Learned

Name _____

Date _____

Guide to My Science Portfolio

My Science Portfolio

What Is in My Portfolio	Why I Chose It
1.	
2.	
3.	
4.	
5.	
6.	
7.	

I organized my Science Portfolio this way because _____
_____
_____
_____
_____

Portfolio Evaluation Checklist

Name _____

Date _____

Portfolio Evaluation

Aspects of Science Literacy	Evidence of Growth
1. **Understands science concepts** (Animals, Plants; Earth's Land, Air, Water; Space; Weather; Matter, Motion, Energy)	
2. **Uses inquiry skills** (observes, compares, classifies, gathers/interprets data, communicates, measures, experiments, infers, predicts, draws conclusions)	
3. **Thinks critically** (analyzes, synthesizes, evaluates, applies ideas effectively, solves problems)	
4. **Displays traits/attitudes of a scientist** (is curious, questioning, persistent, precise, creative, enthusiastic; uses science materials carefully; is concerned for environment)	

Summary of Portfolio Assessment

For This Review			Since Last Review		
Excellent	Good	Fair	Improving	About the Same	Not as Good

AG xxiv   Assessment Guide   Grade 3

Name _____
Date _____

Chapter Assessment

Getting Ready for Science

Vocabulary

Match each term in Column B with its meaning in Column A.

Column A

___ 1. A test done to find out whether a hypothesis is correct

___ 2. The one thing in a scientific test that is different

___ 3. The study that a scientist does

___ 4. An organized plan that scientists use to conduct a study

___ 5. A possible answer to a question

___ 6. A tool used to pick up and hold on to objects

___ 7. The questioning or close study of something

___ 8. To come up with a plan or a model

Column B

A. formulate
B. inquiry
C. hypothesis
D. forceps
E. variable
F. scientific method
G. experiment
H. investigation

Science Concepts

Write the letter of the best choice.

___ 9. Which tool would you use to measure the distance around the trunk of a tree?
   A. hand lens
   B. measuring tape
   C. ruler
   D. thermometer

Name _____

___ **10.** Which of these is **not** an inquiry skill?
   F. coloring   **H.** measuring
   G. comparing   **J.** predicting

___ **11.** What would you use this tool to measure?
   A. mass of a solid
   B. weight of a solid
   C. volume of a liquid
   D. temperature of a liquid

___ **12.** Which is the first step in the scientific method?
   F. draw a conclusion
   G. plan an experiment
   H. form a hypothesis
   J. observe and ask questions

___ **13.** Suppose you use two balls of different sizes to represent Earth and the moon. What inquiry skill do you use?
   A. classify
   B. formulate models
   C. predict
   D. use time/space relationships

___ **14.** Miguel made a graph showing how many students have blue or brown eyes. What inquiry skill did he use?
   F. infer
   G. order
   H. display data
   J. make a prediction

Name _____

___ 15. Which tool would you use to see the parts of a ladybug up close?
  A. forceps
  B. hand lens
  C. measuring tape
  D. thermometer

___ 16. David is using the scientific method to study how plants grow. In one step, he identifies variables and lists the equipment he will use. What is he doing in this step?
  F. gathering data
  G. planning an experiment
  H. drawing a conclusion
  J. investigating further

___ 17. Mara needs to measure a small amount of powder. Which tool should she use?

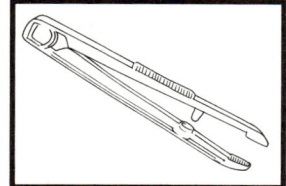

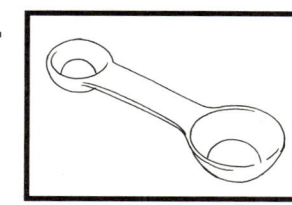

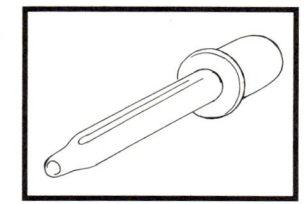

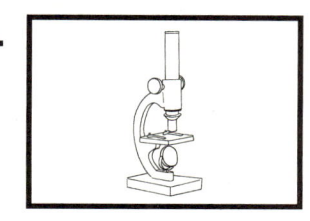

  A.   C.

  B.   D.

___ 18. Which statement is a good hypothesis?
  F. Bubbles are round.
  G. Some bubbles are very big.
  H. Bubbles are fun to look at and play with.
  J. A flexible wand makes better bubbles than a stiff wand.

Getting Ready for Science

Name _____

Critical Thinking

19. What inquiry skills are necessary for planning an experiment?

_____

_____

_____

20. You wish to investigate why some objects float and others do not. Write a hypothesis you could test. Then write a simple plan for an experiment to test your hypothesis.

_____

_____

_____

_____

_____

_____

_____

Name _____
Date _____

Chapter Assessment

Types of Living Things

Vocabulary

Match each term in Column B with its meaning in Column A.

Column A

___ 1. The changes that happen to an organism during its life

___ 2. Passed on from parents

___ 3. A tiny building block that makes up every part of an organism

___ 4. An organism, wrapped in a chrysalis, that doesn't move or eat

___ 5. Series of changes in appearance

___ 6. Any living thing

Column B

A. organism

B. life cycle

C. metamorphosis

D. inherited

E. cell

F. pupa

Science Concepts

Write the letter of the best choice.

___ 7. Which of the following is an example of how a living thing is different from a nonliving thing?
A. Nonliving things reproduce.
B. Living things don't move.
C. Living things reproduce.
D. Nonliving things breathe.

___ 8. What do all living things use to grow?
F. air
G. energy
H. heat
J. skin

Unit A • Chapter 1 (page 1 of 4) Assessment Guide AG 1

Name _____

___ 9. What type of cells keep a plant in the ground?
   A. leaf
   B. root
   C. skin
   D. stem

___ 10. Which do you use to look at a cell?
   F. binoculars
   G. magnifying glass
   H. microscope
   J. thermometer

___ 11. Look at the picture. What part of the cell is the arrow pointing to?
   A. chloroplast
   B. cell membrane
   C. cytoplasm
   D. vacuole

___ 12. What part of the cell tells the cell how to do its job?
   F. cell membrane
   G. cytoplasm
   H. nucleus
   J. vacuole

___ 13. What does a plant cell have that an animal cell does not have?
   A. cell membrane
   B. cell wall
   C. nucleus
   D. vacuole

___ 14. How do tulips and daffodils begin their life cycles?
   F. bulb
   G. seed
   H. stem
   J. tuber

___ 15. Which sequence is correct in the life cycle of an organism?
   A. birth, reproduction, growth, death
   B. birth, death, reproduction, growth
   C. birth, growth, reproduction, death
   D. growth, reproduction, birth, death

Name _____

___ **16.** Which is an inherited trait?
 F. learning to talk
 G. having brown eyes
 H. learning to ride a bike
 J. having several hobbies

Inquiry Skills

17. Lisa plants a seed in soil in a pot. Then she places the pot inside her bedroom closet. She waters the seed every other day for a week. **Infer** what will happen to the seed in a week. Explain.

_____

_____

_____

18. Megan has two dogs. One is a female and the other is a male. Both dogs have white fur and blue eyes. If the dogs have a puppy, **infer** what the puppy will look like. Explain.

_____

_____

_____

_____

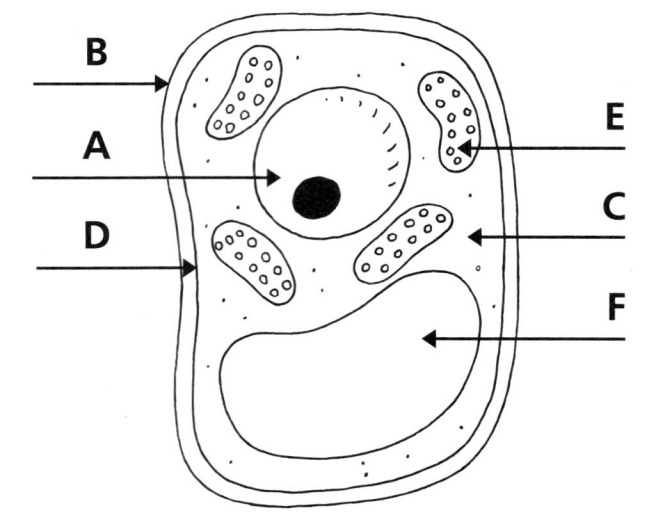

Name _____

Critical Thinking

19. A grasshopper goes through an incomplete metamorphosis. A butterfly goes through a complete metamorphosis. Use these insects to explain the difference between an incomplete metamorphosis and a complete metamorphosis.

_____
_____
_____
_____
_____
_____
_____

20. Label the parts of the plant cell.

A. _____

B. _____

C. _____

D. _____

E. _____

F. _____

Name _____

Date _____

Performance Assessment

Student Task

Life Cycles

Materials

index cards

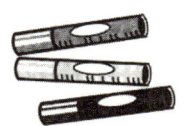

crayons or markers

Procedure

1 Choose one of these plants or animals.

bean plant	beetle	butterfly
chicken	dog	fish
flowering plant	frog	grasshopper
ladybug	snake	turtle

2 Look up the life cycle of your plant or animal.

3 Draw each stage on a separate index card.

4 Label each card with the stage. On the back of the card, write what happens at that stage.

5 Use your picture cards to explain the life cycle of your plant or animal to the class.

Unit A • Chapter 1

Assessment Guide AG 5

Life Cycles

Performance Assessment
Teacher's Directions

Materials Performance Task sheet, index cards, crayons or markers

Time 30 minutes

Suggested Grouping individuals or pairs

Inquiry Skills compare, sequence, communicate

Preparation Hints Obtain cards, or cut 5 in. x 8 in. pieces of white construction paper.

Introduce the Task Review the list of plants and animals with students.

Promote Discussion Remind students to use their picture cards as they explain each stage in the life cycle of their plant or animal. When all students have finished, discuss some of the life cycles that were presented, highlighting their similarities and differences.

Scoring Rubric

Performance Indicators

_____ Draws picture cards and labels them correctly.

_____ Uses the appropriate number of cards to represent the life cycle.

_____ Selects the correct card—in order—when explaining each stage.

_____ Verbally demonstrates an understanding of the life cycle.

Observations and Rubric Score

3   2   1   0

AG 6 Assessment Guide

Unit A • Chapter 1

Name _____
Date _____

Chapter Assessment

Types of Plants

Vocabulary

Match each term in Column B with its meaning in Column A.

Column A

___ 1. The first stage of life for many plants

___ 2. The food factory in a plant

___ 3. The plant part that connects the roots to the leaves

___ 4. The substance that helps plants turn energy from the sun into food

___ 5. A plant that loses its leaves each year

___ 6. The part of a plant that grows underground

___ 7. The process a plant uses to make food

___ 8. A plant that makes food all year long

Column B

A. stem
B. seed
C. evergreen
D. root
E. leaf
F. deciduous
G. photosynthesis
H. chlorophyll

Science Concepts

Write the letter of the best choice.

___ 9. Which of these things does a plant need to live?
 A. fertilizer   C. warmth
 B. oxygen   D. water

___ 10. Plants can live almost anywhere on Earth. What is one way for a desert plant to have enough water?
 F. It loses its leaves in the winter.
 G. It stores water in a thick stem.
 H. It catches water with its leaves.
 J. It uses its water only at night.

Unit A • Chapter 2

Name _____

___ **11.** Which of these do plants need to make food?
   A. oxygen
   B. seeds
   C. soil
   D. sunlight

___ **12.** Which is a way scientists classify plants?
   F. by leaf type
   G. by seed color
   H. by stem length
   J. by root color

___ **13.** If a plant does not make a flower, where could it make a seed?
   A. in the stem
   B. in a root
   C. in a cone
   D. in the leaf

___ **14.** How are all seeds alike?
   F. They are all the same color.
   G. They are all flat and pointed.
   H. They all come from spores or cones.
   J. They all look different from the plants they become.

___ **15.** What kind of food do plants make during photosynthesis?
   A. carbon dioxide
   B. light
   C. sugar
   D. water

___ **16.** What do plants take in during photosynthesis?
   F. carbon dioxide
   G. oxygen
   H. soil
   J. sugar

Name _____

Inquiry Skills

17. Three identical plants were planted in the same kind of soil. The first plant was watered three times every day for two weeks. The second plant was watered once every two days. The third plant was watered once a week. Scientists often **compare** the results they get in their experiments. How would you compare the plants to decide which one received the right amount of water?

_____

_____

_____

18. Two plants were planted in the same type of soil. One was placed in the closet, and one was placed on a sunny windowsill. They were given equal amounts of water for two weeks. **Predict** which plant will be healthier. Explain.

_____

_____

_____

Critical Thinking

19. A dandelion grows from seeds. The featherlike seeds are blown away by the wind. How can a dandelion growing in the schoolyard be a parent to young dandelion plants growing miles from school?

_____

_____

_____

Name _____

20. The pictures show two different plants. How are Plant A and Plant B alike? How are they different?

Plant A   **Plant B**

_____
_____
_____
_____
_____
_____
_____

AG 10   Assessment Guide   (page 4 of 4)   Unit A • Chapter 2

Name _____

Date _____

Performance Assessment

Student Task

Photosynthesis Comic Strip

Materials

crayons or colored pencils

paper

Procedure

Draw a comic strip that shows the process of photosynthesis. Your main character should be a plant that needs food energy. What does the plant need to make its food? What happens as the plant makes its food? Be sure to show the steps of photosynthesis in the correct order.

Do these things to draw your comic:

❶ Make a list of what happens during photosynthesis. Think about the order in which the steps happen. Number the steps.

❷ Draw a comic strip, and show a frame for each step.

- Show the setting, or where the action takes place. Think about the kinds of places where plants live.
- Show your main character, the plant. The plant needs energy and will get energy from photosynthesis.
- Your characters can say things. Use balloons to show what they say.

❸ Give your comic strip a title.

Be sure to use these words when you write your comic strip:

| sun | leaf | chlorophyll | oxygen | carbon dioxide | sugar |

Unit A • Chapter 2   Assessment Guide   AG 11

Photosynthesis Comic Strip

Performance Assessment
Teacher's Directions

Materials Performance Task sheet, crayons or colored pencils, paper

Time 30 minutes

Suggested Grouping individuals or small groups

Inquiry Skills communicate, make models, classify

Preparation Hints You might have small groups of students work on large pieces of butcher paper. If so, move desks or rearrange the room to allow space for students to work.

Introduce the Task Review with students the process of photosynthesis. Prompt students, if necessary, to use the words that appear in the word box. After reviewing photosynthesis, let students know that they will design a comic strip in which a plant with little energy gets more energy from photosynthesis. Students' comic strips can be funny or serious. Students can add other characters and dialogue to their comic strips. The strips should reflect the following main points: the leaf combines carbon dioxide and water to make sugar for the plant; oxygen is released into the air; chlorophyll in the leaf captures light energy, which powers the process.

Promote Discussion When students finish, invite them to share their comic strips with classmates. Extend the discussion by having students trace the steps of photosynthesis in other students' or groups' comic strips.

Scoring Rubric

Performance Indicators

_____ Draws a comic strip that shows how photosynthesis gives energy to a plant.
_____ Puts the steps in the correct order.
_____ Shows a setting that takes into account the needs of plants.
_____ Shows key vocabulary in the comic strip: *sun, leaf, chlorophyll, oxygen, carbon dioxide, sugar.*

Observations and Rubric Score

3   2   1   0

Name _____

Date _____

Chapter Assessment

Types of Animals

Vocabulary

Match each term in Column B with its meaning in Column A.

Column A

___ 1. An animal with feathers and wings

___ 2. An animal with dry, scaly skin

___ 3. An animal with moist skin and no scales

___ 4. An animal that has a backbone

___ 5. A gas animals need that is found in air and water

___ 6. An animal that has no backbone

___ 7. An animal with gills that lives in the water

___ 8. An animal with fur or hair that makes milk for its young

Column B

A. oxygen

B. vertebrate

C. mammal

D. bird

E. fish

F. amphibian

G. reptile

H. invertebrate

Science Concepts

Write the letter of the best choice.

___ 9. Which is something that **all** animals need?
  A. fur
  B. lungs
  C. oxygen
  D. warmth

___ 10. Which animal is a reptile?
  F. bear
  G. bird
  H. monkey
  J. snake

Unit A • Chapter 3   (page 1 of 4)   Assessment Guide   AG 13

Name _____

___ 11. Which is a trait of **all** birds?
   A. They can all fly.
   B. They are all born with gills.
   C. They all hatch from eggs.
   D. They all feed their young milk.

___ 12. Which animals are in the same group?
   F. crocodile and snake
   G. frog and worm
   H. ladybug and shark
   J. spider and fish

___ 13. Which animal has no backbone?

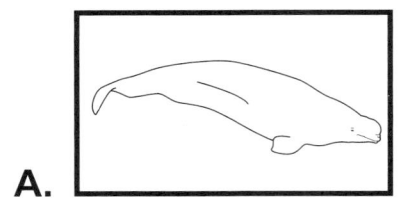

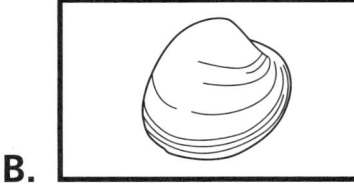

A. [whale]   C. [lizard]

B. [clam]   D. [snake]

___ 14. Which of these is **not** a trait of mammals?
   F. have hair or fur
   G. have scales
   H. feed milk to their young
   J. breathe with lungs

___ 15. How are insects and spiders alike?
   A. They both have eight legs.
   B. They both are vertebrates.
   C. They both have an outer body covering.
   D. They both have two body parts.

Name _____

___ 16. Josh's brother made this table to help Josh learn about animals.

Type of Animal	Trait
amphibian	has gills as an adult
bird	lives on land and under water
fish	has feathers
reptile	has skin with scales

He told Josh that only one kind of animal is correctly paired with its trait. Which kind is this?

F. amphibian   H. mammal
G. fish   J. reptile

Inquiry Skills

17. Animals have characteristics that make them part of a group. **Compare** and **contrast** reptiles and amphibians.

_____
_____
_____

18. A scientist finds an animal's nest. The nest has pieces of eggshell and feathers. **Infer** what this animal is and how it will get from place to place. Explain.

_____
_____
_____
_____

Name _____

Critical Thinking

19. Circle the animal that is **most** unlike the others. Then tell why you chose this animal.

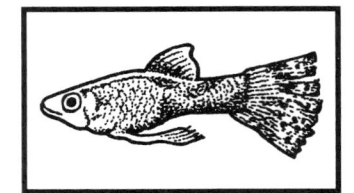

_____
_____
_____
_____

20. A friend tells you that frogs and fish belong to the same group of animals because they can both live in a pond. Do you agree or disagree? Explain.

_____
_____
_____
_____

Name _____

Date _____

Performance Assessment

Student Task

Classify Animals

Materials

index cards   crayons or markers   construction paper   glue

Procedure

1 Think of five animals that belong to different groups. Draw pictures of these animals on index cards. Write each animal's name on the card.

2 For each animal you drew, write the name of the group it belongs to on another index card. Use one of these words: *mammal, reptile, amphibian, bird,* or *fish.*

3 For each animal you drew, write on a third index card some traits it has that show why the animal belongs to its group.

4 Glue the index cards for each animal on a sheet of construction paper in a column, as shown here.

5 Share your work with the class.

Unit A • Chapter 3   Assessment Guide   **AG 17**

Classify Animals

Performance Assessment
Teacher's Directions

Materials Performance Task sheet, index cards, crayons or markers, construction paper, glue

Time 30 minutes

Suggested Grouping pairs

Inquiry Skills compare, classify

Preparation Hints Count out index cards for students. If index cards are not available, you might cut cards from construction paper. Instead of having students draw pictures of animals, you might provide animal pictures from magazines. Be sure the pictures include a wide variety of animals representing all five groups.

Introduce the Task Explain to students that they will be drawing and classifying animals. You may wish to briefly review lesson content about animal groups. Distribute the Performance Task sheets, and read the directions with students. Make certain students understand how they are to arrange their index cards.

Promote Discussion Remind students to include animals from all five groups. If necessary, suggest examples to students during the card preparation period. Remind students that their lists of traits must be those used to classify animals into major groups. For example, *bats can fly* does not explain why bats are mammals. When students share their work, ask them to justify their classifications and their lists of traits.

Scoring Rubric

Performance Indicators

_____ Makes cards showing an animal from each group.

_____ Correctly classifies the animals into their major groups.

_____ Writes appropriate traits for the animal groups.

_____ Explains the reasoning behind the classifications and trait lists.

Observations and Rubric Score

3   2   1   0

Assessment Guide   Unit A • Chapter 3

Name _____

Date _____

Unit Assessment

Write the letter of the best choice.

____ 1. What is the difference between living and nonliving things?
   A. Living things reproduce.
   B. Nonliving things reproduce.
   C. Nonliving things need energy.
   D. Living things do not need energy.

____ 2. What kind of food do plants make?
   F. green
   G. salt
   H. sugar
   J. water

____ 3. Jason found a long, thin, needle-like leaf. From what type of tree did the leaf probably come?
   A. apple
   B. maple
   C. oak
   D. pine

____ 4. What do all animals need in order to survive?
   F. food, warmth, sun, and eggs
   G. food, water, shelter, and oxygen
   H. sun, food, warmth, and shelter
   J. water, hair, food, and air

____ 5. Which is **not** an ordinary way for water to leave your body?
   A. in your breath
   B. in your sweat
   C. in your urine
   D. in your blood

Unit A

Name _____

___ 6. What do all plants need in order to survive?
    F. air, light, and shade
    G. soil, roots, and weeds
    H. soil, water, air, and light
    J. water, grass, and sun

___ 7. What is the first stage of growth for plants?
    A. birth
    B. eggs
    C. leaves
    D. seeds or spores

___ 8. What body part or parts does this animal use to help it get food?

    F. its ears
    G. its feet
    H. its skin
    J. its trunk

___ 9. How do insects get oxygen?
    A. from the water
    B. through their antennae
    C. by breathing air through gills
    D. through tiny holes in their bodies

Name _____

___ 10. In what part of a plant is food made?
   F. flower
   G. leaf
   H. root
   J. stem

___ 11. Joey has an animal that has moist skin, lays eggs in water, and has lungs. Which type of vertebrate is it most likely to be?
   A. amphibian
   B. bird
   C. fish
   D. reptile

___ 12. What kind of shelter do beavers build?
   F. burrows
   G. dams
   H. lodges
   J. nests

___ 13. What do all invertebrates have in common?
   A. All have lots of legs.
   B. All have simple bodies.
   C. None have backbones.
   D. None have wings.

___ 14. What part of the plant is the arrow pointing to?
   F. flower
   G. leaf
   H. root
   J. stem

Unit A

Name _____

___ 15. To what group of vertebrates does a whale belong?
    A. amphibian
    B. fish
    C. mammal
    D. reptile

___ 16. What do fish use to help them breathe?
    F. fins
    G. gills
    H. scales
    J. tail

___ 17. Which of the following is the beginning of a life cycle?
    A. a bean
    B. birth
    C. death
    D. a root

___ 18. What does this picture show?
    F. camouflage
    G. instinct
    H. metamorphosis
    J. migration

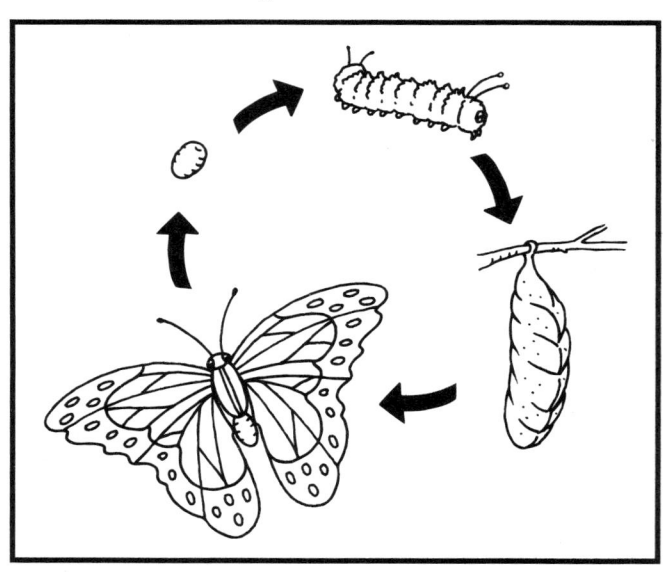

Name _____

___ **19.** Which is true about insects?
   A. They all have wings.
   B. They all have four legs.
   C. They all have six body parts.
   D. There are more of them than of any other kind of animal.

Write the answer to each question.

20. Is this a picture of an animal cell or a plant cell? How can you tell?

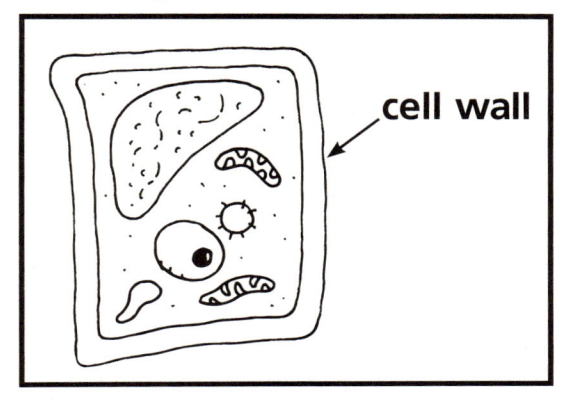

cell wall

_____
_____
_____

21. Melissa planted a seed in the soil in a cave. Will the plant grow? Why or why not?

_____
_____

Name _____

22. List three ways people use plants.

_____

_____

_____

23. Grandma put earthworms in her garden. Did this help or harm her garden? Explain.

_____

_____

_____

Name _____
Date _____

Chapter Assessment

Where Living Things Are Found

Vocabulary

Match each term in Column B with its meaning in Column A.

Column A

___ 1. A group of organisms of the same kind living in the same place

___ 2. Go into a sleeplike state for the winter

___ 3. The living and nonliving things that surround a living thing

___ 4. The living and nonliving things that interact in an environment

___ 5. Imitating the look of another animal

___ 6. Any trait that helps an animal survive

___ 7. All of the populations that live in an ecosystem at the same time

___ 8. The place where a population lives in an ecosystem

Column B

A. community
B. habitat
C. adaptation
D. population
E. hibernate
F. mimicry
G. environment
H. ecosystem

Science Concepts

Write the letter of the best choice.

___ 9. Which of the following live in a coniferous forest?
  A. deciduous trees   C. monkeys
  B. jaguars   D. pine trees

Unit B • Chapter 4　　(page 1 of 4)　　Assessment Guide　　AG 25

Name _____

___ 10. In warm weather, little brown bats live in trees. When it gets cold, they move to caves, where it is warmer. What is this an example of?
   F. camouflage   H. migration
   G. hibernation   J. mimicry

___ 11. Which is a natural event that can change an ecosystem?
   A. flooding   C. mimicry
   B. hibernation   D. road building

___ 12. How do people help ecosystems?
   F. by building houses
   G. by planting trees
   H. by making roads
   J. by using water

___ 13. What kind of adaptation does the animal in the picture have?

   A. mimicry   C. instinct
   B. hibernation   D. camouflage

___ 14. Which is an example of an instinct?
   F. a parrot says "hello"
   G. a dolphin jumps through a hoop
   H. a dog barks on command
   J. a snake cools off in the shade

___ 15. Which is a nonliving part of an environment?
   A. animals   C. rocks
   B. plants   D. trees

AG 26 Assessment Guide   (page 2 of 4)   Unit B • Chapter 4

Name _____

___ **16.** Of which type of ecosystem is most of Earth made up?
   F. desert
   G. freshwater
   H. grassland
   J. saltwater

Inquiry Skills

17. Devon is hiking in the Mojave Desert. **Predict** what things he might observe there. Give an example of two living and two nonliving things.

_____
_____
_____

18. Compare the physical features of these two animals. What can you **infer** about how each is adapted to its environment?

jackrabbit   arctic hare

_____
_____
_____

Unit B • Chapter 4   (page 3 of 4)   Assessment Guide   AG 27

Name _____

Critical Thinking

19. How can damage to an ecosystem harm animals that live there?

_____

_____

_____

_____

20. Jason is making a poster about ecosystems. He is showing grassland, desert, coniferous forest, and saltwater ecosystems. He has the following pictures of plants and animals that he needs to place in the correct ecosystems.

Match each plant or animal with the ecosystem that best fits its needs.

_____

_____

_____

Name _____

Date _____

Performance Assessment

Student Task

Ecosystem Mobile

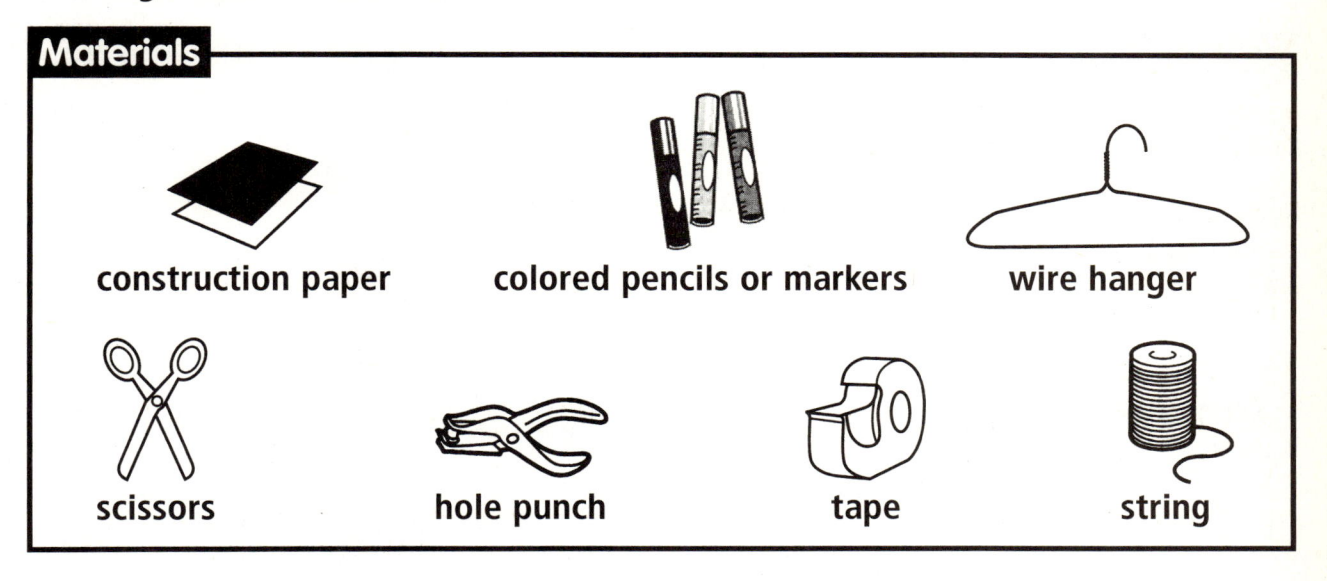

Materials

- construction paper
- colored pencils or markers
- wire hanger
- scissors
- hole punch
- tape
- string

Procedure

Choose and model an ecosystem.

1. Choose an ecosystem described in the chapter. Write a description of its plants and animals.

2. On the construction paper, draw and color pictures of the plants and animals in the ecosystem you chose. Cut out the pictures. Lay them out to show how you would group them.

3. Make an ecosystem mobile by attaching string to your pictures and hanging them from the hanger in groups.

4. Cut out a piece of construction paper about the size of a small index card. On the paper, write the name of the ecosystem and some key words that describe it. Hang it from the hanger.

5. Share your mobile with the class. Describe the ecosystem shown by your mobile.

Unit B • Chapter 4

Assessment Guide AG 29

Ecosystem Mobile

Performance Assessment
Teacher's Directions

Materials Performance Task sheet, construction paper, colored pencils or markers, wire hanger, scissors, hole punch, tape, string

Time 40–50 minutes

Suggested Grouping pairs

Inquiry Skills observe, classify, compare

Preparation Hints Ask students to bring a wire coat hanger from home. Instead of drawing pictures, students may cut out pictures from old magazines. Provide students with additional source material about a variety of ecosystems.

Introduce the Task Ask students to recall characteristics of certain ecosystems. Tell them they are going to choose an ecosystem and research it. They will write a description of the ecosystem and draw or cut out pictures of plants and animals that live there. Explain to students that they will then construct a mobile to display the relationships among organisms in the ecosystem.

Promote Discussion Have student pairs display their mobiles, explaining which ecosystems they chose and the plants and animals found there. Compare the mobiles after all student pairs have made their presentations.

Scoring Rubric

Performance Indicators

_____ Researches an ecosystem, and draws or selects plants and animals that are part of the ecosystem.

_____ Appropriately groups plants and animals that inhabit the ecosystem.

_____ Accurately lists key words that describe the ecosystem.

_____ Accurately explains the characteristics of the ecosystem represented by the mobile.

Observations and Rubric Score

| 3 | 2 | 1 | 0 |

AG 30 Assessment Guide

Unit B • Chapter 4

Name _____
Date _____

Chapter Assessment

Living Things Depend on One Another

Vocabulary

Match each term in Column B with its meaning in Column A.

Column A

____ 1. A living thing that breaks down dead things for food

____ 2. A consumer that eats only plants

____ 3. Overlapping food chains

____ 4. A living thing that makes its own food

____ 5. Shows the path of food from one living thing to another

____ 6. An animal that hunts another animal for food

____ 7. A consumer that gets its food by eating other animals

____ 8. A living thing that gets energy by eating other living things as food

Column B

A. consumer
B. food web
C. carnivore
D. predator
E. decomposer
F. food chain
G. herbivore
H. producer

Science Concepts

Write the letter of the best choice.

____ 9. Which of these is a decomposer?
  A. bee   C. grass
  B. earthworm D. plant

____ 10. Which of the following would a herbivore eat?
  F. berries   H. rabbits
  G. mice   J. worms

Unit B • Chapter 5   (page 1 of 4)   Assessment Guide   AG 31

Name _____

___ **11.** In which group does a grizzly bear belong?
    A. carnivore   **C.** herbivore
    B. decomposer   **D.** omnivore

___ **12.** Which is the producer in this simple food chain?

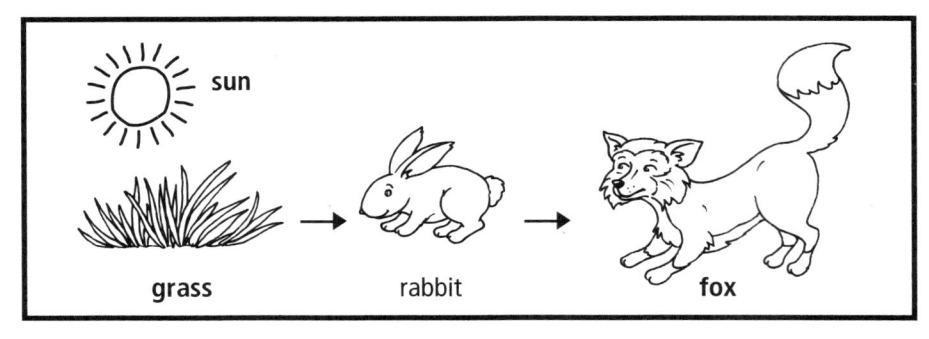

    F. fox   **H.** rabbit
    G. grass   **J.** sun

___ **13.** Hawks are predators. Which of the following is the hawk's prey?
    A. an insect   **C.** an octopus
    B. a mouse   **D.** a tiger

___ **14.** How might a food web change if a new plant were added?
    F. There might be fewer animals.
    G. The new plant might crowd out other plants.
    H. There might be a decrease in herbivores.
    J. There might be a decrease in carnivores.

___ **15.** This diagram shows how energy is used in a food chain. What is this diagram called?

    A. energy grid   **C.** energy chain
    B. energy pyramid   **D.** food web

Name _____

___ 16. Which is **not** an example of how prey can hide from predators?
   F. biting their own tails
   G. squirting ink and hiding behind it
   H. having a body shaped like a leaf or a stick
   J. using their own color to blend in with the environment

Inquiry Skills

17. Sarah has these picture sorting cards. She needs to arrange the cards **to make a model** of how these things might interact in a food chain. Tell the order of these organisms in a food chain.

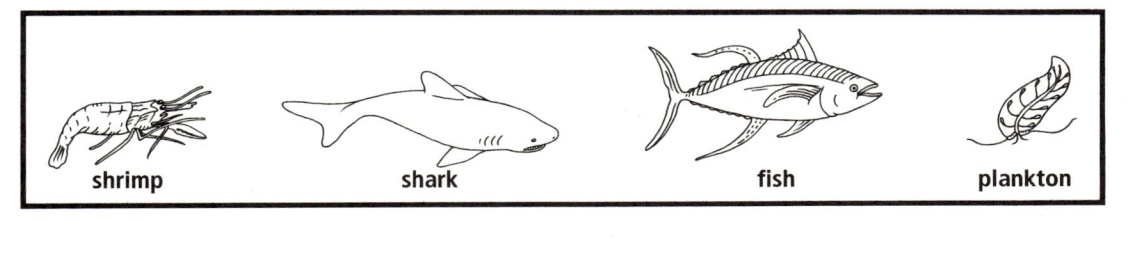

| shrimp | shark | fish | plankton |

_____
_____
_____
_____

18. Living things depend on one another. **Communicate** what would happen if all the producers on Earth died.

_____
_____

Name _____

Critical Thinking

19. Look at this food chain. What would happen if the birds became extinct?

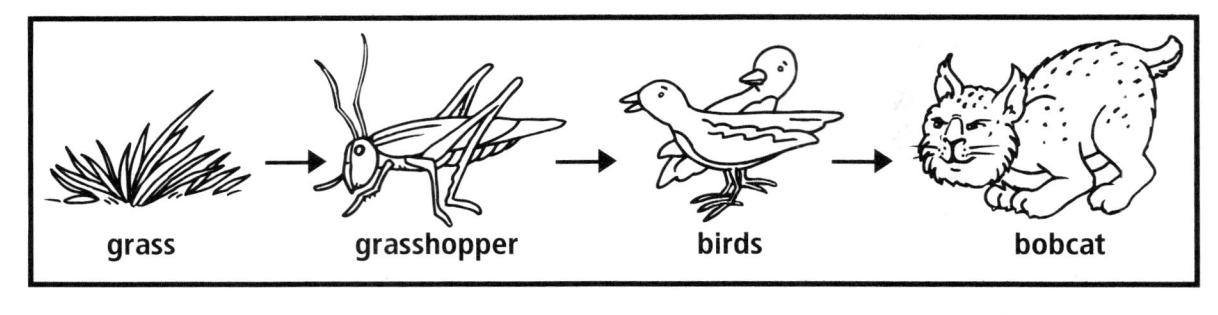

grass → grasshopper → birds → bobcat

_____
_____
_____
_____

20. You eat several different things, so you are part of many food chains. Think about what you ate today. Tell about a food chain that includes one of the foods you ate.

_____
_____
_____

Name _____

Date _____

Performance Assessment

Student Task

Your Food Web

Materials

pencil

markers

Procedure

Use the space below to draw your food web in pencil before finishing it with the markers.

Design a food web that includes everything you eat in a normal day. Show what the organisms in your web eat that you also eat. Also show what the organisms eat that you do **not** eat. Share your completed food web with the class. Explain the relationships among the organisms in your web.

Unit B • Chapter 5

Your Food Web

Performance Assessment
Teacher's Directions

Materials Performance Task sheet, pencil, markers

Time 30 minutes

Suggested Grouping groups of two or three

Inquiry Skills classify, communicate, infer

Preparation Hints On the board, draw a food chain that results in a hamburger. Include a cow and grass.

Introduce the Task Read the directions and the task description as the students follow along. Make the food chain you drew on the board into a food web. Add food chains that include other foods found in typical school lunches. Connect the food chains wherever there are shared elements (for example, cheese comes from milk, milk comes from cows, hamburgers are made from cows). The outer part of the food web should show the foods students eat. The inner part of the food web should show the things that make up those foods.

Promote Discussion As groups explain their food webs, ask them if every food chain should include a producer.

Scoring Rubric

Performance Indicators

_____ Draws a food web showing the foods that the student eats.

_____ Compares the food web with those of others.

_____ Explains the relationships among the organisms in the web.

Observations and Rubric Score

| 3 | 2 | 1 | 0 |

Name _____

Date _____

Unit Assessment

Write the letter of the best choice.

___ 1. What is formed by the living and nonliving things that interact in an environment?
   A. a community
   B. an ecosystem
   C. a habitat
   D. a population

___ 2. Which of these would be the first in a food chain?

   F. acorn
   G. fox
   H. squirrel
   J. fox and squirrel

___ 3. Which would you most likely find in an ocean?
   A. bison
   B. cactus
   C. cattails
   D. coral

___ 4. What do you call overlapping food chains?
   F. energy cycles
   G. energy pyramid
   H. food web
   J. producers

Name _____

___ 5. Which would **not** cause a change in a food web?
   A. a sunny day
   B. a decrease in plants
   C. adding a new animal
   D. an increase in plants

___ 6. Which are consumers?
   F. bacteria
   G. trees
   H. mushrooms
   J. tigers

___ 7. A cow has flat teeth. What does this tell you about cows?
   A. They are carnivores.
   B. They are producers.
   C. They are herbivores.
   D. They are decomposers.

___ 8. What do you call all the frogs that live in a pond?
   F. a habitat
   G. a community
   H. a population
   J. an environment

___ 9. Which make up Earth's largest ecosystem?
   A. deserts
   B. forests
   C. lakes
   D. oceans

___ 10. Wolves hunt rabbits. What are the rabbits in this situation?
   F. consumer
   G. predator
   H. prey
   J. producer

Name _____

____ 11. Which of the following is true about deserts?
　　　　A. There is no animal life.
　　　　B. They are dry ecosystems.
　　　　C. The plants need lots of water.
　　　　D. The temperature is always mild.

____ 12. Which is an example of camouflage?
　　　　F. Whales go to Alaska.
　　　　G. A bear sleeps through the winter.
　　　　H. A lizard blends in with a green leaf.
　　　　J. A nonharmful snake looks like a harmful snake.

____ 13. Where do pine and fir trees grow?
　　　　A. rain forest
　　　　B. desert
　　　　C. coniferous forest
　　　　D. deciduous forest

____ 14. In what habitat would you most likely find this animal?

　　　　F. forest
　　　　G. ocean
　　　　H. pond
　　　　J. rain forest

Unit B　　　　Assessment Guide

Name _____

____ 15. Which is the biggest group in an energy pyramid?
   A. decomposers
   B. herbivores
   C. omnivores
   D. producers

Use the picture to answer Questions 16–17.

____ 16. Which is the producer in this food chain?
   F. deer
   G. grass
   H. vulture
   J. wolf

____ 17. Which is the decomposer in this food chain?
   A. bacteria
   B. grass
   C. vulture
   D. wolf

____ 18. Which of the following includes a baby fish's knowing how to swim?
   F. adaptations
   G. hibernation
   H. instincts
   J. migration

Name _____

___ **19.** A chimpanzee eats fruits and insects. Which of the following terms describes the chimpanzee?
   A. carnivore
   B. decomposer
   C. herbivore
   D. omnivore

Write the answer to each question.

20. How can damage to an ecosystem harm animals that live there?

_____

_____

_____

21. If an animal has both flat and sharp teeth, what conclusion can be made about the food it eats?

_____

_____

_____

22. Explain how the loss of a forest might affect a food chain.

_____

_____

_____

Name _____

23. Prey animals have ways of defending themselves against predators. These ways sometimes keep them from being caught and eaten. What effect do these ways have on a food web?

_____

_____

_____

_____

Name _____
Date _____

Chapter Assessment

Minerals and Rocks

Vocabulary

Match each term in Column B with its meaning in Column A.

Column A

___ 1. Rock that was once melted and then cooled and hardened

___ 2. Rock that has been changed by heat and pressure

___ 3. Rock formed from material that has settled into layers

___ 4. An object that is solid, formed in nature, and has never been alive

___ 5. The remains of a living thing that died long ago

___ 6. A naturally formed solid made of one or more minerals

Column B

A. rock

B. sedimentary rock

C. igneous rock

D. fossil

E. mineral

F. metamorphic rock

Science Concepts

Write the letter of the best choice.

___ 7. What do you call the color of the powder left behind by a mineral when it's rubbed against a rough white tile?
 A. hematite C. rock
 B. quartz D. streak

___ 8. What properties are used to identify a mineral?
 F. shape and streak H. hardness, streak, and color
 G. size and streak J. color, shape, and hardness

Unit C • Chapter 6 (page 1 of 4) Assessment Guide AG 43

Name _____

____ 9. What are the three layers of Earth?
   A. center, middle, outer   C. core, mineral, center
   B. core, mantle, crust   D. mantle, inner, outer

____ 10. What type of rock is formed from volcanoes?
   F. igneous   H. sandstone
   G. metamorphic   J. sedimentary

____ 11. What does this picture show?

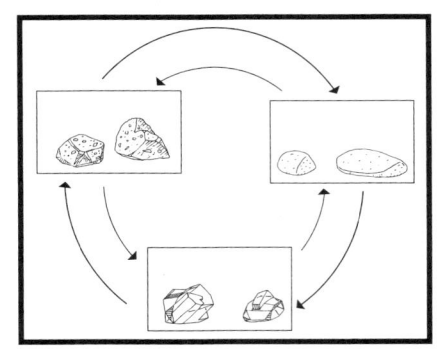

   A. how sediments build up
   B. types of soil
   C. rock cycle
   D. igneous rock

____ 12. Which is an imprint fossil?
   F. bones   H. shells
   G. dinosaur tracks J. teeth

____ 13. What can scientists infer by finding this fossil?

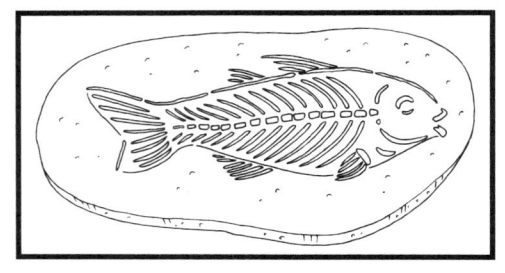

   A. the kind of food the animal ate
   B. that a sea once covered the area
   C. what animals are like today
   D. what ate this kind of animal

AG 44   Assessment Guide   (page 2 of 4)   Unit C • Chapter 6

Name _____

___ **14.** Which of the following is **not** a mineral?
    F. diamond   **H.** granite
    G. gold   **J.** quartz

___ **15.** Why are plant fossils not as common as animal fossils?
    A. Plants don't have teeth.
    B. Plants are smaller than animals.
    C. There were more animals than plants.
    D. The soft parts of plants are easily destroyed.

___ **16.** What is formed when mud or minerals fill a mold?
    F. cast   **H.** rock
    G. fossil   **J.** wood

Inquiry Skills

17. Tim needs to create a science fair project. His mother suggested that he **make and use a model** of a fossil. Tim wants to make a mold and cast a fossil. How can he do this?

_____
_____
_____
_____
_____

Unit C • Chapter 6   (page 3 of 4)   Assessment Guide   AG 45

Name _____

18. Knowing the hardness of a mineral can help you identify it. The Mohs scale below tells the hardness of a mineral. Use it to write the correct **order** from hardest to softest for the following minerals: topaz, fluorite, talc, calcite, diamond, and quartz.

1 Talc	2 Gypsum	3 Calcite	4 Fluorite	5 Apatite
6 Orthoclase feldspar	7 Quartz	8 Topaz	9 Corundum	10 Diamond

_____

_____

Critical Thinking

19. Why are most fossils found in sedimentary rock?

_____

_____

_____

_____

20. Mrs. Smith's class has a collection of rocks. If igneous rock were kept in the classroom for six months, would it change into metamorphic rock? Why or why not?

_____

_____

_____

_____

Assessment Guide

Unit C • Chapter 6

Name _____
Date _____

Performance Assessment

Student Task

Building Rocks

Materials

modeling clay (variety of colors)

index cards

assorted small objects

Procedure

1. Using different colors of clay, make models of igneous rock, metamorphic rock, and sedimentary rock.

2. Think about the kind of rock that would contain the remains of animals or plants that lived long ago. Place some of the small objects in your model of this rock.

3. Label each rock with an index card.

4. On the back of the card, tell why you made the rock look the way it does.

5. Think about how people use each type of rock. On a separate card, write the name of the rock on one side. On the other side, tell what you might build or make with this type of rock.

Unit C • Chapter 6

Assessment Guide   AG 47

Building Rocks

Performance Assessment
Teacher's Directions

Materials Performance Task sheet, modeling clay (variety of colors), index cards, assorted small objects

Time 30 minutes

Suggested Grouping pairs or small groups

Inquiry Skills use models, observe, infer

Preparation Hints none

Introduce the Task Explain to students that they are going to make models of different types of rock. You may need to guide students to realize that the assorted small objects can be used to represent fossils. Review differences among rock types by showing pictures or samples of different kinds of rocks.

Promote Discussion After students finish, encourage them to share their work with the class. Ask them to explain their lists of ways people use each type of rock.

Scoring Rubric

Performance Indicators

_____ Builds accurate models of igneous, metamorphic, and sedimentary rock.

_____ Accurately labels the index cards and lists specific characteristics for each rock.

_____ Infers that fossils could be found in sedimentary rock.

_____ Lists appropriate ways that each type of rock can be used.

Observations and Rubric Score

| 3 | 2 | 1 | 0 |

Name _____

Date _____

Chapter Assessment

Forces That Shape the Land

Vocabulary

Match each term in Column B with its meaning in Column A.

Column A

___ 1. An opening on Earth's surface from which lava flows

___ 2. A flat area higher than the land around it

___ 3. A large amount of water that covers normally dry land

___ 4. The movement of weathered rock and soil

___ 5. The way rocks are broken down into smaller pieces

___ 6. The shaking of Earth's surface

___ 7. A valley with steep sides

___ 8. A huge block of ice

Column B

A. earthquake
B. plateau
C. glacier
D. volcano
E. canyon
F. flood
G. weathering
H. erosion

Science Concepts

Write the letter of the best choice.

___ 9. Which of the following does **not** cause weathering?
   A. plant roots
   B. soil
   C. water
   D. wind

Unit C • Chapter 7   Assessment Guide   AG 49

Name _____

___ **10.** Which of the following is a very slow type of erosion that moves rocks and soil?
    F. creep   **H.** landslide
    G. fault   **J.** volcano

___ **11.** What does this illustration show?
    A. canyon
    B. glacier
    C. plateau
    D. valley

___ **12.** What causes a flood?
    F. drought
    G. landslides
    H. gas and ash that erupt from a volcano
    J. heavy rainfall that makes rivers overflow

___ **13.** Where can you find beaches?
    A. canyon   **C.** Great Plains
    B. coastal plains   **D.** mountains

___ **14.** What is a butte?
    F. a deep canyon
    G. a table made of rock
    H. a flat-topped hill with steep sides
    J. a rocky mountain

___ **15.** Which of the following causes sand dunes?
    A. earthquakes   **C.** landslides
    B. rain   **D.** wind

___ **16.** Which of these causes a quick change to the land?
    F. erosion   **H.** weathering
    G. volcano   **J.** wind

Name _____

Inquiry Skills

17. Compare a plateau with a footstool. How are they alike?

_____

_____

18. Look at the two bars of the graph. **Interpret the data** to explain how the change happened.

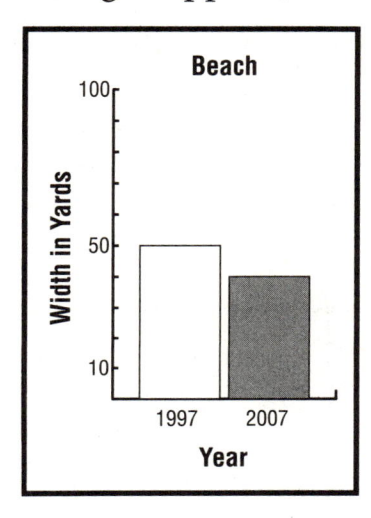

Beach

Width in Yards

100
50
10

1997   2007

Year

_____

_____

_____

Name _____

Critical Thinking

19. Imagine you are examining an old map of a town you are visiting. The map is hundreds of years old. You notice that the river today is not where it is on the map. Is this possible? Explain.

_____
_____
_____
_____

20. In which of these three areas could a landslide happen? Explain your answer.

A	B	C
desert	mountains	lake

_____
_____
_____
_____

Name _____
Date _____

Performance Assessment

Student Task

Erosion

Materials

- aluminum foil
- shoe box with lid
- 4 cups of soil
- water
- measuring cup
- dried leaves and twigs

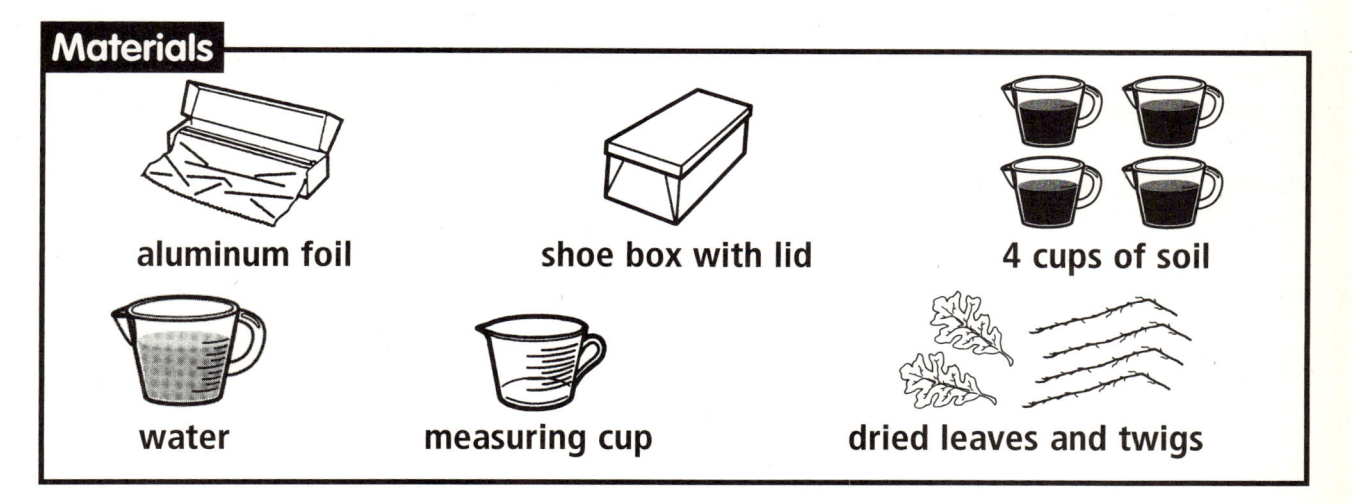

Procedure

1. Line the shoe box with foil. Then wrap the lid with foil, and place the lid in the box to make a ramp.

2. If the soil is not damp, add a little water to make it damp.

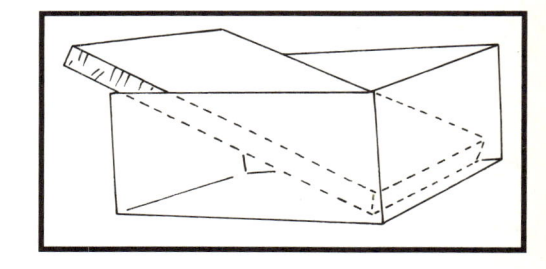

3. Spread half of the soil to cover the ramp. Crumble the dried leaves and twigs, and mix them into the rest of the soil. Put that soil aside.

4. Pour 1 cup of water along the top edge of the ramp as slowly as you can.

   What happens to the soil? _____

5. Clear away the plain soil. Then spread the soil with the leaf and twig bits in it on the ramp. Again pour 1 cup of water very slowly along the top edge of the ramp.

   What happens to the soil? _____

6. What can you infer from your observations?

Unit C • Chapter 7

Assessment Guide   AG 53

Erosion

Performance Assessment
Teacher's Directions

Materials Performance Task sheet, aluminum foil, shoe box with lid, soil, water, measuring cup, dried leaves and twigs

Time 30 minutes

Suggested Grouping pairs or small groups

Inquiry Skills make a model, observe, interpret data, infer

Preparation Hints Make sure the soil is damp before giving it to students. Provide newspaper to cover tables, and use large trash bags for easy cleanup.

Introduce the Task Explain to students that they will make a model to show how water erodes soil. Have students carefully read the directions for the task and then follow them.

Promote Discussion Encourage students to discuss their observations. Ask them what they can infer from their observations.

Scoring Rubric

Performance Indicators

_____ Creates the erosion box.

_____ Conducts the task with both types of soil.

_____ Explains the results of the task by stating that the plain soil eroded to a much greater degree than the soil containing leaves and twigs.

_____ Infers that things that anchor the soil help prevent erosion.

Observations and Rubric Score

| 3 | 2 | 1 | 0 |

Name _____
Date _____

Chapter Assessment

Conserving Resources

Vocabulary

Match each term in Column B with its meaning in Column A.

Column A

____ 1. Saving resources by using them wisely

____ 2. To use less of things

____ 3. Any harmful material in the environment

____ 4. To break down or change a product and use it to make something new

____ 5. A material that is found in nature and is used by living things

____ 6. To use again and again

____ 7. A resource that can be used again and again

____ 8. The part of soil made up of dead plants and animals

Column B

A. humus
B. recycle
C. resource
D. reusable resource
E. pollution
F. conservation
G. reduce
H. reuse

Science Concepts

Write the letter of the best choice.

____ 9. Which resource is found below ground?
   A. air
   B. cotton
   C. gasoline
   D. oil

Unit C • Chapter 8   (page 1 of 4)   Assessment Guide   AG 55

Name _____

___ **10.** Which of the following resources is renewable?
  F. coal   **H.** soil
  G. gasoline   **J.** trees

___ **11.** Which layer of soil is the arrow pointing to?
  A. bedrock
  B. clay soil
  C. subsoil
  D. topsoil

___ **12.** What can cause pollution in the air and on land to get into water?
  F. cars   **H.** rain
  G. factories   **J.** water treatments

___ **13.** You use the same skis that are now too small for your older brother. What are you doing?
  A. recycling resources   **C.** reinventing resources
  B. reducing resources   **D.** reusing resources

___ **14.** Which product can be made from recycled plastic?
  F. cans   **H.** greeting cards
  G. doormats   **J.** newspaper

___ **15.** Which is **not** mined from the land?
  A. coal   **C.** gold
  B. gemstones   **D.** wood

Name _____

___ **16.** What type of soil is made up of powdery grains of rock?
   F. humus   **H.** clay
   G. loam   **J.** sand

Inquiry Skills

17. Compare the two pictures. In which place would you **infer** that people need to conserve water? Why?

_____
_____

18. Compare what it means to reduce use of resources and to reuse resources. Give an example of each.

_____
_____
_____
_____
_____

Name _____

Critical Thinking

19. Karen learned that water is a reusable resource. She was told that water used to wash dishes or clothes can be reused. The thought of reusing that water did not seem like a good idea to her. What makes it possible to reuse this water? Explain your answer.

_____

_____

_____

20. Frances wants to grow tomatoes. The area that she chose for her tomato plants has clay soil. Why would this area not be good for growing tomatoes? If she must plant the tomatoes there, what can she do to prepare the soil?

_____

_____

_____

_____

Name _____
Date _____

Performance Assessment

Student Task

Treasure Trash

Materials

poster board   markers

Procedure

Make a table showing how some of the things we throw away could be recycled or reused or both.

1 List six things that are often thrown away but that could be recycled or reused or both.

_____   _____

_____   _____

_____   _____

2 Make a four-column chart on your poster board. Label the columns TRASH, RECYCLE, REUSE, and HOW THIS HELPS.

3 Fill in the TRASH column with things from your list.

4 With your group, decide if each item could be recycled. If it could, mark an X in the RECYCLE column. Then brainstorm ways each item might be reused. Tell how in the REUSE column.

5 In the last column, tell how recycling or reusing the items will help conserve resources.

6 Share your chart with the class.

Unit C • Chapter 8   Assessment Guide   AG 59

Treasure Trash

Performance Assessment — Teacher's Directions

Materials Performance Task sheet, poster board, markers

Time 30–40 minutes

Suggested Grouping small groups

Inquiry Skills communicate

Preparation Hints You may wish to help students create the chart they will use to record their thoughts.

Introduce the Task Write on the board the names of one or two items that are commonly thrown away. Have students decide whether each item you listed could be recycled. Then have them brainstorm ways each could be reused. Help them think of other items commonly thrown away that could be recycled or reused or both. List their suggestions on the board, and allow groups to draw from the list for their charts.

Promote Discussion Display the finished charts in the classroom. Encourage each group to choose one of its items and elaborate on how it could be reused and how this would help conserve resources. Ask students to summarize what they have learned about recycling and reusing to conserve resources.

Scoring Rubric

Performance Indicators

_____ Creates a chart that lists items of trash that can be recycled or reused.

_____ Presents practical ways of reusing the items.

_____ Communicates ideas clearly.

_____ Expresses understanding of how conservation helps save resources.

Observations and Rubric Score

3   2   1   0

Name _____
Date _____

Unit Assessment

Write the letter of the best choice.

____ 1. Which is **not** a property of a mineral?
   A. color
   B. hardness
   C. streak
   D. temperature

____ 2. Which is a way to cut down on pollution?
   F. drive cars
   G. walk to school
   H. dump oil in the ocean
   J. throw trash on the street

____ 3. Which is a nonrenewable resource?
   A. animals
   B. soil
   C. trees
   D. water

____ 4. What are Earth's highest landforms?
   F. canyons
   G. mountains
   H. plains
   J. valleys

____ 5. What are the three main layers of Earth?
   A. center, crust, mantle
   B. crust, mantle, core
   C. crust, middle, outer
   D. mantle, inner, outer

Name _____

___ 6. What type of landform is found in the middle of the United States?
    F. beaches
    G. glaciers
    H. plains
    J. valleys

___ 7. What four things make up soil?
    A. water, sand, dirt, and seeds
    B. fossils, humus, water, and dirt
    C. air, grain, dirt, and tiny pieces of rock
    D. water, air, humus, and tiny pieces of rock

___ 8. What is the process that moves pieces of rock and soil?
    F. erosion
    G. delta
    H. mudslide
    J. weathering

___ 9. In which of the following would you be most likely to find a fossil?
    A. lava rock
    B. igneous rock
    C. sedimentary rock
    D. metamorphic rock

___ 10. What is formed when mud or minerals fill a mold?
    F. bone
    G. cast
    H. rock
    J. soil

Name _____

___ 11. Rock that melts, cools, and hardens becomes what type of rock?
   A. igneous
   B. marble
   C. metamorphic
   D. sedimentary

___ 12. Which of the following can help clean the air?
   F. plants, wind, and rain
   G. cars, gasoline, and rain
   H. trees, factories, and plants
   J. cars, exhaust, and factories

___ 13. What causes erosion?
   A. heat
   B. cold
   C. sun and water
   D. wind or water

___ 14. Which of these is an effect of an earthquake?
   F. areas covered with lava
   G. gas clouds
   H. burned forests
   J. uneven areas of ground

___ 15. What type of soil is primarily found on farms?
   A. clay
   B. dirt
   C. loam
   D. rocks

Name _____

___ 16. What type of fossil does this picture show?

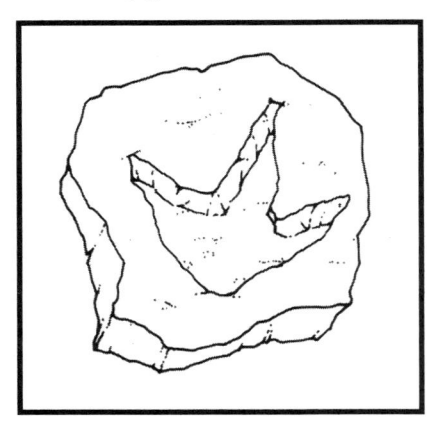

    F. cast
    G. imprint
    H. mold
    J. plant

___ 17. What do you call an opening on Earth's surface from which hot, melted rock flows?

    A. ash
    B. crust
    C. soil
    D. volcano

___ 18. What type of resource is a plant?

    F. reusable resource
    G. renewable resource
    H. refundable resource
    J. nonrenewable resource

Name _____

____ **19.** Which lists the soils in order from biggest to smallest grains?
   A. clay, sand, silt
   B. clay, silt, sand
   C. sand, clay, silt
   D. sand, silt, clay

Write the answer to each question.

20. How do floods help farmers?

_____
_____
_____

21. Why do few fossils form in metamorphic and igneous rock?

_____
_____
_____

22. Why is it important to protect renewable resources such as air and water?

_____
_____
_____

Name _____

23. Does weathering occur in areas that have freezing temperatures? How do you know?

_____

_____

_____

Name _____
Date _____

Chapter Assessment

The Water Cycle

Vocabulary

Match each term in Column B with its meaning in Column A.

Column A

___ 1. Rain, snow, sleet, or hail

___ 2. The air around Earth

___ 3. Earth's underground supply of water

___ 4. The change of a gas into a liquid

___ 5. Water that has very little salt in it

___ 6. The movement of water from Earth's land and water into the air and back again

___ 7. The change of a liquid into a gas

___ 8. A huge sheet of ice

Column B

A. fresh water

B. glacier

C. groundwater

D. condensation

E. evaporation

F. precipitation

G. water cycle

H. atmosphere

Science Concepts

Write the letter of the best choice.

___ 9. Cheryl's mom is getting ready to cook pasta. When the water boils, which process will occur?
  A. condensation
  B. evaporation
  C. melting
  D. precipitation

___ 10. A radio announcer tells you it's a sunny day and the temperature is 70° F. What is the announcer describing?
  F. the atmosphere
  G. the ocean
  H. the water cycle
  J. the weather

Unit D • Chapter 9   Assessment Guide   AG 67

Name _____

___ 11. Trevor sees white, wispy clouds high in the sky. Which type of cloud is Trevor seeing?
   A. cirrus   C. rain
   B. cumulus   D. stratus

___ 12. Why is groundwater important?
   F. Groundwater warms the land.
   G. People can find groundwater easily.
   H. Groundwater contains more salt than ocean water.
   J. People use groundwater for drinking and bathing.

___ 13. Luis is observing ice cubes as they change. He drew this picture.

   What does the picture show?
   A. boiling   C. melting
   B. freezing   D. precipitation

___ 14. Water moves from the air to the land, through rivers to the ocean, and back to the air. How does water move from the air to the land?
   F. It falls as precipitation.
   G. It forms as groundwater.
   H. It evaporates from the sky.
   J. It forms glaciers in Antarctica.

___ 15. Which of these processes forms clouds?
   A. Water vapor expands as it rises.
   B. Solid water evaporates.
   C. Liquid water freezes.
   D. Water vapor rises and condenses.

___ 16. What does an anemometer measure?
   F. wind speed   H. cloud height
   G. temperature   J. rainfall amount

Name _____

Inquiry Skills

Lindsay collected weather data for three days. She recorded the data in a table. Use the table to answer Questions 17–18.

Data	Day 1	Day 2	Day 3
Temperature	85°F	82°F	75°F
Precipitation	None	None	Rain

17. **Infer** why the temperature was cooler on Day 3.

_____

_____

_____

18. Suppose Lindsay had also wanted to **record** the types of clouds she saw. What type of cloud would Lindsay have recorded on Day 3? Why?

_____

_____

_____

Name _____

Critical Thinking

19. Why do scientists measure precipitation?

_____

_____

_____

20. At 8 A.M., snow covers the ground and icicles hang from gutters. At 1 P.M., the snow is melting and the icicles are dripping. What must have happened to the temperature during these five hours? Explain.

_____

_____

_____

_____

_____

Name _____

Date _____

Performance Assessment

Student Task

What's the Weather?

Materials

pencil

Procedure

1 Your teacher will provide you with a weather map or a weather page from a newspaper. Use this information to complete Day 1 of the table.

2 Do this again for Day 2 and Day 3.

	Day 1	Day 2	Day 3
Temperature			
Weather conditions			
Precipitation			

Predict what the weather will be like on Day 4. Explain your prediction.

_____

_____

_____

Unit D • Chapter 9

Assessment Guide   AG 71

What's the Weather?

Performance Assessment
Teacher's Directions

Materials Performance Task sheet, pencil, weather map or other printed weather information

Time 10–15 minutes per day, 20 minutes on the last day

Suggested Grouping pairs or groups

Inquiry Skills observe, record, predict, communicate

Preparation Hints Make certain you have sufficient source material for the three-day period. Acquaint students with the weather page from a local newspaper or other source. Show them how to find the information asked for in the table. Decide whether students should record amounts of precipitation, or merely the presence of precipitation. You may also wish to specify the phrases students will use to describe weather conditions—for example: *sunny, partly cloudy, cloudy, rainy* or *snowy*.

Introduce the Task Pass out the Performance Task sheets, and read the directions with students. Explain that they will complete the table over a three-day period. Clarify the kinds of information students will record in the table.

Promote Discussion After the task is completed, ask students to judge the accuracy of their forecasts. Point out that other kinds of weather information could have been recorded. Ask students whether they think this additional information would have helped them to more accurately predict the weather on Day 4. In summary, ask students to make a generalization about how difficult it is to predict the weather accurately.

Scoring Rubric

Performance Indicators

_____ Locates required weather data in source material.

_____ Accurately records weather data for each day.

_____ Makes a reasonable prediction of the weather for Day 4.

_____ Uses the collected data to justify the prediction.

Observations and Rubric Score

3   2   1   0

Name _____

Date _____

Chapter Assessment

Earth's Place in the Solar System

Vocabulary

Match each term in Column B with its meaning in Column A.

Column A

____ 1. The imaginary line Earth rotates around

____ 2. Pattern of phases of the moon

____ 3. The sun and the planets and other objects circling it

____ 4. A time when the moon's shadow falls on Earth

____ 5. A large body of rock or gases that revolves around the sun

____ 6. A group of stars that form a picture

____ 7. A hot ball of glowing gases

____ 8. The movement of a planet around the sun

Column B

A. constellation
B. axis
C. lunar cycle
D. star
E. planet
F. revolution
G. solar system
H. solar eclipse

Science Concepts

Write the letter of the best choice.

____ 9. Light rays from the sun heat Earth. Which kind of light rays causes Earth to get the warmest?
  A. bent light rays
  B. curved light rays
  C. slanted light rays
  D. straight light rays

____ 10. Which of these is at the center of the solar system?
  F. Earth
  G. moon
  H. planet
  J. sun

Unit D • Chapter 10   (page 1 of 4)   Assessment Guide   AG 73

Name _____

| A | B | C | D |

___ **11.** Which picture above shows the season when the rays from the sun are striking Earth at the greatest slant?
   A. A
   B. B
   C. C
   D. D

___ **12.** Which is **not** true of the inner planets?
   F. The inner planets have rocky surfaces.
   G. The inner planets are made mostly of gases.
   H. The inner planets are warmer than the outer planets.
   J. The inner planets are smaller than the outer planets.

___ **13.** In which way are Earth and Mars alike?
   A. Both planets have a watery surface.
   B. The length of a day is about the same.
   C. The distance across is about the same.
   D. The length of a year is about the same.

___ **14.** About how long is the lunar cycle?
   F. 7 days   **H.** 35 days
   G. 29 days   **J.** 365 days

___ **15.** Which is an inner planet?
   A. Earth   **C.** Saturn
   B. Jupiter   **D.** Neptune

Name _____

___ **16.** What causes a lunar eclipse?
  F. The moon changes from new moon to full moon.
  G. The sun blocks moonlight from reaching Earth.
  H. The moon blocks sunlight from reaching Earth.
  J. The Earth blocks sunlight from reaching the moon.

Inquiry Skills

17. Ivan found a table that showed the size across of some planets in kilometers. Based on this table, in which **order** should Ivan place the planets so that they are arranged from smallest to largest?

Planet	Size
Mercury	4,800 km
Venus	12,100 km
Earth	12,800 km
Mars	6,800 km

_____

_____

18. Olivia found a **model** of Earth and the sun. Based on this **model**, which seasons in North America are shown by positions A, B, C, and D?

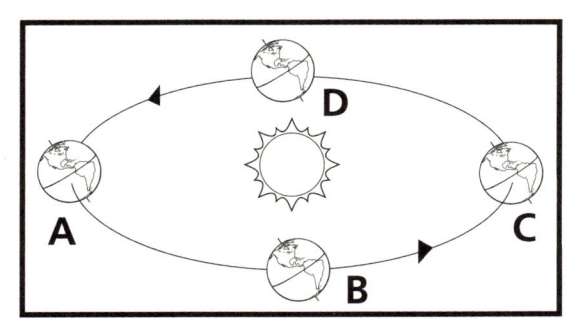

_____

_____

Unit D • Chapter 10   (page 3 of 4)   Assessment Guide   AG 75

Name _____

Critical Thinking

19. It takes Earth 365 days to revolve around the sun. If Earth revolved around the sun once every 730 days, what would happen to the length of each season?

_____

_____

_____

20. You have found the following diagram of the solar system. Based on this diagram, is it possible that any objects could run into each other if they keep moving in their orbits? Explain.

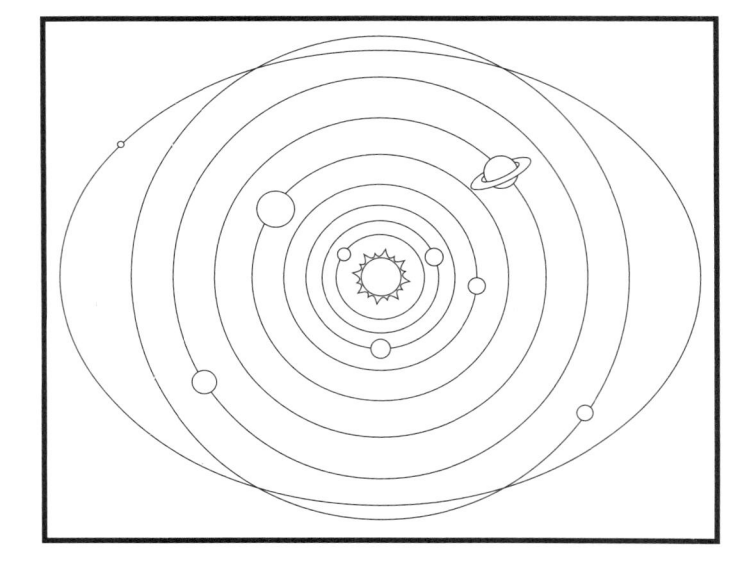

_____

_____

_____

Name _____

Date _____

Performance Assessment

Student Task

Earth's Seasons

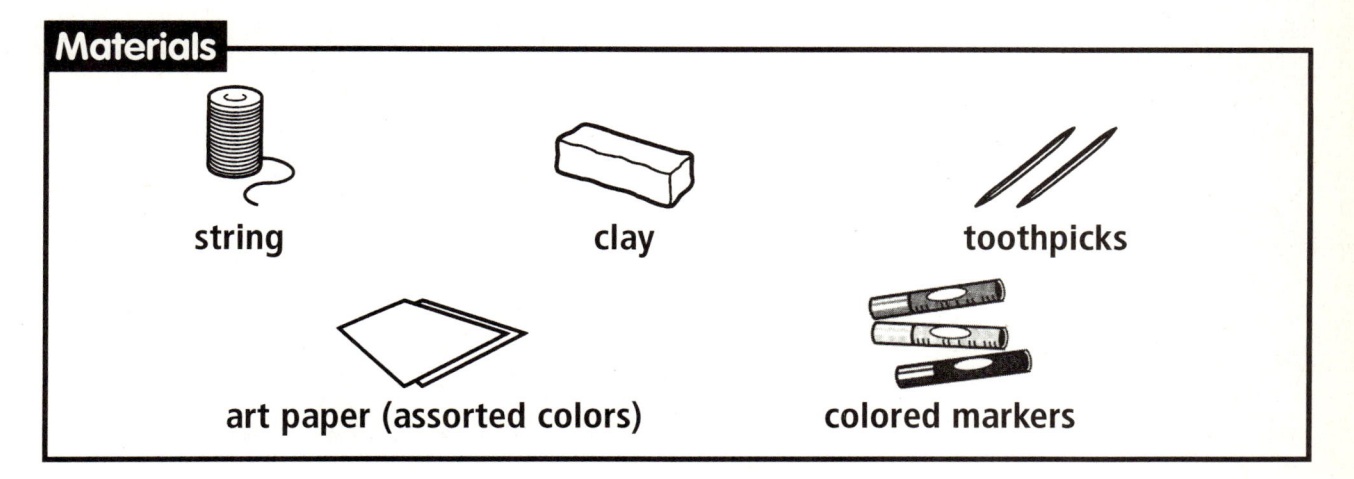

Materials

- string
- clay
- toothpicks
- art paper (assorted colors)
- colored markers

Procedure

Make a model to show why Earth has seasons.

❶ What will you use to represent the sun? _____

❷ What will you use to represent Earth and its axis? _____

❸ What will you use to show the path Earth travels around the sun?

_____

❹ Make a mark on your model to show about where you live on Earth. Now place Earth so that its North Pole is tilted toward the sun.

Would it be summer or winter where you live? _____

❺ Move Earth around the sun. Keep the tilt of its axis the same all the way around. When the South Pole is tilted toward the sun, would it be summer or winter where you live?

_____

❻ Add labels to your model to show Earth's position in orbit during each season. Share your model with the class. Using your model, tell why Earth has seasons.

Unit D • Chapter 10   Assessment Guide   AG 77

Earth's Seasons

Performance Assessment
Teacher's Directions

Materials Performance Task sheet, string, clay, toothpicks, art paper (assorted colors), colored markers

Time 30 minutes

Suggested Grouping groups of two or three

Inquiry Skills make a model, observe, infer, compare, communicate

Preparation Hints You may wish to provide additional materials for students to use in making their models.

Introduce the Task Ask students to tell what they know about seasonal changes in weather. Have a student hold a globe to represent Earth on its axis, while you hold a bright light to represent the sun. Ask a volunteer to point out on the globe about where all of you live.

Promote Discussion Have volunteers tell how the student with the globe should move to represent Earth's movement around the sun. Check at various points to see that the tilt of the axis stays the same. Discuss how Earth's changing position affects the way in which sunlight strikes Earth's surface. Urge students to relate this to seasonal changes as they explain their models to the class.

Scoring Rubric

Performance Indicators

_____ Selects appropriate objects or materials to represent the sun, Earth on its axis, and Earth's orbit around the sun.

_____ Demonstrates how Earth moves in orbit around the sun without changing the tilt of its axis.

_____ Makes a model to show the position of Earth during the four seasons of the year.

_____ Relates seasonal changes to changes in the way sunlight strikes Earth's surface.

Observations and Rubric Score

3   2   1   0

Name _____
Date _____

Unit Assessment

Write the letter of the best choice.

____ 1. What is the path in which a planet revolves?
   A. a galaxy
   B. an orbit
   C. a revolution
   D. a solar system

____ 2. What happens to water in a pot if the water is left to boil for a long time?
   F. The water level rises.
   G. The water gets cooler.
   H. The water changes from a solid to a gas.
   J. The water changes from a liquid to a gas.

____ 3. What instrument would a meteorologist use to measure wind speed?
   A. anemometer
   B. map
   C. satellite
   D. thermometer

____ 4. In which of the following can salt water be found in all three places?
   F. oceans, gulfs, and seas
   G. ponds, lakes, and rivers
   H. gulfs, streams, and rivers
   J. streams, ponds, and oceans

____ 5. About how long does it take Earth to revolve around the sun?
   A. 365 hours
   B. 365 days
   C. 36 days
   D. 1 day

Unit D   (page 1 of 6)   Assessment Guide   AG 79

Name _____

___ 6. Which form is water in when it is water vapor?
    F. gas
    G. heat
    H. liquid
    J. solid

___ 7. Which of the following can be used to predict weather?
    A. map
    B. microscope
    C. rain gauge
    D. weather satellite

___ 8. What is the spinning of Earth on its axis?
    F. poles
    G. revolution
    H. rotation
    J. tilt

___ 9. Which moon phase is shown?

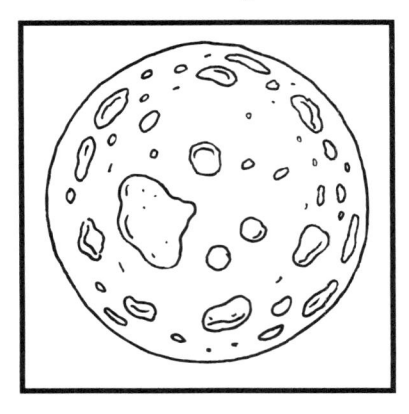

    A. first quarter   **C.** new moon
    B. full moon   **D.** third quarter

___ 10. Where is almost all of the fresh water on Earth found?
    F. Africa
    G. Antarctica
    H. Asia
    J. Europe

Name _____

___ 11. The state that water is in depends on which of the following?
   A. clouds
   B. temperature
   C. vapor
   D. volume

___ 12. What type of cloud is shown?

   F. circular
   G. cirrus
   H. cumulus
   J. stratus

___ 13. What happens when light rays strike at a slant?
   A. The day ends.
   B. There is no light.
   C. The light is brighter.
   D. The light rays spread out more.

___ 14. By which process are clouds formed?
   F. condensation
   G. evaporation
   H. melting
   J. precipitation

Name _____

___ **15.** What happens during a lunar eclipse?
　　　A. Earth blocks light from reaching the sun.
　　　B. The moon blocks light from reaching Earth.
　　　C. The moon blocks light from reaching the sun.
　　　D. Earth blocks light from reaching the moon.

___ **16.** What type of water is only a small part of the water on Earth?
　　　F. clear
　　　G. fresh
　　　H. salt
　　　J. sea

___ **17.** When it is summer, what can you infer about the sun's rays?
　　　A. They are weak.
　　　B. There are none.
　　　C. They are at a slant.
　　　D. They are striking directly.

___ **18.** What does this picture show?

　　　F. glacier
　　　G. groundwater
　　　H. seasons
　　　J. water cycle

AG 82　Assessment Guide　(page 4 of 6)　Unit D

Name _____

___ **19.** How long does it take Earth to rotate once?
   A. one day
   B. one month
   C. one year
   D. one hour

Write the answer to each question.

20. Compare the inner planets to the outer planets. How are they alike? How are they different?

_____

_____

_____

_____

_____

21. If there were no water on Earth, there also would be no snow. Explain this statement.

_____

_____

_____

Name _____

22. Raymond has a small red ball, a medium-size blue ball, and a desk lamp. What should he do with the materials to model a lunar eclipse?

_____

_____

_____

23. How can predicting the chance and amount of rainfall be helpful to people?

_____

_____

_____

_____

Name _____
Date _____

Chapter Assessment

Properties of Matter

Vocabulary

Match each term in Column B with its meaning in Column A.

Column A

___ 1. The amount of matter in something

___ 2. Matter with a volume and shape that stay the same

___ 3. The mass of matter compared to its volume

___ 4. A mixture in which different kinds of matter mix evenly

___ 5. Matter with no definite shape or volume

___ 6. Anything that takes up space

___ 7. The amount of space matter takes up

___ 8. Matter with a volume that stays the same but a shape that changes

Column B

A. density
B. gas
C. matter
D. solid
E. mass
F. liquid
G. solution
H. volume

Science Concepts

Write the letter of the best choice.

___ 9. Which of the following is matter that you cannot see?
   A. air
   B. clouds
   C. ice
   D. water

Unit E • Chapter 11   (page 1 of 4)   Assessment Guide   AG 85

Name _____

___ 10. Kevin needs to measure the mass of an apple. What tool can he use?
    F. a balance   H. a ruler
    G. a barometer   J. a thermometer

___ 11. Which group of words names physical properties of matter?
    A. mirror, wool, cotton   C. sour, green, hot
    B. salt, candy, sugar   D. tall, building, glass

___ 12. Which of the following groups names three states of matter?
    F. gas, oil, water   H. solid, liquid, gas
    G. liquid, water, ice   J. solid, penny, liquid

___ 13. Which of the following has the greatest density?

    A. cotton balls   C. jelly beans

    B. feathers   D. rocks

___ 14. Mica makes a salad of oranges, apples, and bananas. What is the bowl of fruit salad an example of?
    F. condensation   H. a mixture
    G. evaporation   J. a solution

___ 15. Which is a chemical change?
    A. burning wood   C. folding paper
    B. cutting cloth   D. mixing salt and water

Name _____

____ **16.** Which of these is a solution?
     F. cereal and milk   **H.** orange and apple slices
     G. ice cream and nuts   **J.** sugar and water

Inquiry Skills

17. Janet knows the mass of some peanuts and the mass of some pretzels. She mixes them together to make trail mix. How can she determine the mass of the trail mix if she doesn't have a tool to **measure** it? Explain.

_____

_____

_____

18. Charlie is testing whether things sink or float. He puts a plastic-foam board in the water. **Predict** whether the board will sink or float. Explain your reasoning.

_____

_____

_____

Unit E • Chapter 11   Assessment Guide

Name _____

Critical Thinking

19. Tyrell had a large bowl of ice cubes. He left the bowl out in the hot sun for a couple of hours. What happened to the ice cubes? Explain.

_____

_____

_____

20. Teresa popped some popcorn and cooked some rice. She measured a cup of each as shown in the pictures.

Compare the volumes of the popcorn and the rice. Then determine which is denser, the popcorn or the rice. Explain.

_____

_____

_____

_____

_____

Name _____
Date _____

Performance Assessment

Student Task

Sink or Float?

Materials

measuring cup    water    several small objects

Procedure

1 Fill the measuring cup three-quarters full with water.

2 Place an object in the water. Does it sink, or does it float? Record your observations in the data table below.

3 Remove the first object from the water. Repeat Step 2 for the other objects. Refill the cup with water if necessary.

4 Review the data you recorded in the table. Which objects are denser than water? Which objects are less dense? Tell how you know.

Object	Sinks	Floats	Denser Than Water	Less Dense Than Water

Unit E • Chapter 11   Assessment Guide   AG 89

Sink or Float?

Performance Assessment — Teacher's Directions

Materials Performance Task sheet, measuring cup, water, several small objects

Time 30 minutes

Suggested Grouping individuals or pairs

Inquiry Skills observe, compare, draw conclusions, communicate

Preparation Hints Gather small objects—some that float and some that sink—for example, marbles, paper clips, coins, leaves, corks, and plastic bottle caps.

Introduce the Task Tell students that they will determine whether some common objects sink or float in water. From this, they will conclude which objects are more dense than water and which are less dense than water.

Promote Discussion When students finish, ask them to share their observations about the objects that sank and those that floated. Were their observations similar? Then review the definition of *density*. Ask students to explain density in terms of the mass of matter in a given volume and to relate this to the objects that sank or floated.

Scoring Rubric

Performance Indicators

_____ Determines whether each object sinks or floats.

_____ Records observations accurately.

_____ Concludes that objects sink or float because they are more dense or less dense than water, respectively.

_____ Understands that density is a relationship between mass and volume.

Observations and Rubric Score

3	2	1	0

Name _____

Date _____

Chapter Assessment

Energy

Vocabulary

Match each term in Column B with its meaning in Column A.

Column A

___ 1. Resource that can be replaced

___ 2. Another word for *burning*

___ 3. The ability to make something move or change

___ 4. The energy of position

___ 5. Resource that cannot be replaced

___ 6. Something in nature that people use

___ 7. The energy of motion

___ 8. Coal, oil, and gas

Column B

A. energy

B. resource

C. combustion

D. fossil fuels

E. renewable resource

F. kinetic energy

G. nonrenewable resource

H. potential energy

Science Concepts

Write the letter of the best choice.

___ 9. Where does most of Earth's energy come from?
   A. electricity
   B. fossil fuels
   C. the moon
   D. the sun

Name _____

___ **10.** What type of energy does a moving car have?
    F. electrical energy   **H.** light energy
    G. kinetic energy   **J.** potential energy

___ **11.** Which of the following is a way to save energy resources?
    A. Use a blanket instead of turning on the heater.
    B. Keep the house cool by turning on the air conditioning.
    C. Turn on the lights during the day.
    D. Leave the light on when you exit a room.

___ **12.** Which of the following are fossil fuels?
    F. coal and natural gas   **H.** light and oil
    G. water and coal   **J.** heat and natural gas

___ **13.** Which resource is renewable?
    A. coal   **C.** oil
    B. gas   **D.** wind

___ **14.** Which ball has **no** kinetic energy?

    F. ball 1   **H.** ball 3
    G. ball 2   **J.** ball 4

Name _____

____ **15.** What kind of energy do plants need to grow?
   A. chemical   **C.** light
   B. electrical   **D.** sound

____ **16.** What tool measures wind energy?
   F. anemometer   **H.** sound meter
   G. light meter   **J.** thermometer

Inquiry Skills

17. Tyler and his sister went to the beach. Tyler sat in the sun, and his sister sat in the shade. **Infer** what happened to each person's skin temperature. Explain.

_____
_____
_____
_____

18. In Molly's town everyone drives a car to go anywhere. People leave their appliances on all the time, use their heaters or air conditioners every day, and do not recycle materials. **Infer** what will happen to the world if everyone acts the way people do in Molly's town.

_____
_____
_____

Name _____

Critical Thinking

19. List five ways that you can conserve energy at home or at school.

_____

_____

_____

_____

20. Carly is sitting at the top of the slide.

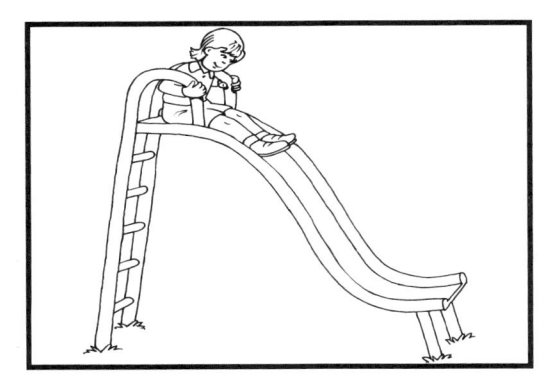

What type of energy does she have? Is it possible for her to change her energy? If she changes her energy, what type of energy will it become? Explain your answers.

_____

_____

_____

_____

Name _____
Date _____

Performance Assessment

Student Task

Types of Energy

Materials

magazines or newspapers   construction paper   glue

scissors

Procedure

1. Choose one of the following types of energy.
   - heat
   - chemical
   - electric
   - mechanical
   - sound
   - light

2. Look through the magazines and newspapers for pictures that show how this type of energy is used.

3. Glue the pictures to a piece of construction paper.

4. Show your pictures to the class, and have the class guess which energy source you chose.

5. Then tell about each picture. Explain how the energy source is being used.

Unit E • Chapter 12   Assessment Guide   AG 95

Types of Energy

Performance Assessment — Teacher's Directions

Materials Performance Task sheet, magazines or newspapers, construction paper, glue, scissors

Time 30 minutes

Suggested Grouping pairs or small groups

Inquiry Skills observe, gather data, interpret data

Preparation Hints If you want to cover each type of energy, divide the class into six groups. Write each type of energy on a slip of paper, and put the slips in a bag. Have each group select a slip.

Introduce the Task Review the list of energy types. Ask students to give an example of how each type is used. Then tell them that they will choose one type of energy and will look through magazines and newspapers for examples of how it is used. Allow students also to draw pictures to illustrate the type of energy being used.

Promote Discussion When students finish, ask them to show their displays to the class. Have the class guess which type of energy is being used in each display. Then have students explain how the energy is being used in each picture.

Scoring Rubric

Performance Indicators

_____ Identifies pictures that show examples of the type of energy chosen.

_____ Makes a display that correctly shows examples of the type of energy chosen.

_____ Shows a variety of examples.

_____ Explains how the type of energy is being used in each example.

Observations and Rubric Score

3   2   1   0

Assessment Guide — Unit E • Chapter 12

Name _____
Date _____

Chapter Assessment

Electricity and Magnets

Vocabulary

Match each term in Column B with its meaning in Column A.

Column A

___ 1. An electric charge that builds up in an object

___ 2. A path that electricity follows

___ 3. Able to attract objects made of iron

___ 4. A machine that uses a magnet to make a current of electricity

Column B

A. circuit
B. static electricity
C. generator
D. magnetic

Science Concepts

Write the letter of the best choice.

___ 5. Which is an example of electricity?
  A. brush
  B. cloud
  C. hair
  D. lightning

___ 6. What kind of electricity moves through a wire?
  F. current
  G. motor
  H. socket
  J. static

___ 7. Which material is a good conductor of electricity for your toaster cord?
  A. copper
  B. insulator
  C. plastic
  D. wood

___ 8. What makes a refrigerator's motor do work to keep food cold?
  F. current electricity
  G. insulator
  H. lightning
  J. static electricity

Unit E • Chapter 13   (page 1 of 4)   Assessment Guide   AG 97

Name _____

___ 9. The graph at the right shows the number of nails four different magnets are able to lift. Which magnet is the strongest?
   A. Magnet I
   B. Magnet II
   C. Magnet III
   D. Magnet IV

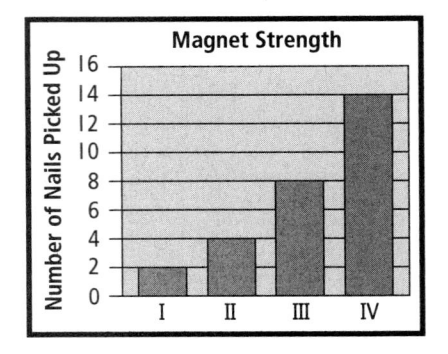

___ 10. What are the ends of magnets called?
   F. attractors   H. poles
   G. north   J. south

___ 11. What is needed to make electricity?
   A. magnet only   C. both a magnet and a coil of wire
   B. coil of wire only D. neither a magnet nor a coil of wire

___ 12. Which diagram shows magnets attracting each other?

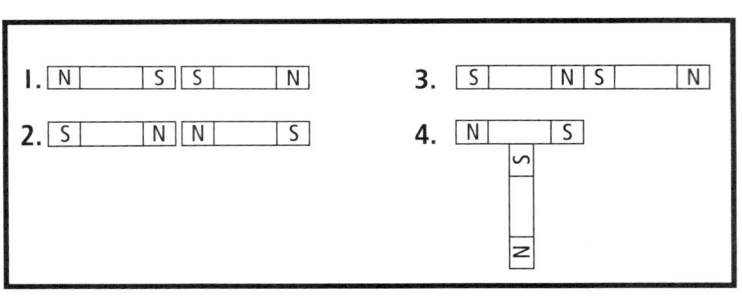

   1. [N   S][S   N]   3. [S   N][S   N]
   2. [S   N][N   S]   4. [N   S]
                                  [S]
                                  [N]

   F. 1   H. 3
   G. 2   J. 4

___ 13. Which is **not** a use for magnets?
   A. to make electicity   C. to sort metal for recycling
   B. to make compasses   D. to separate glass from plastic

___ 14. What can magnets do to a piece of iron?
   F. repel it   H. turn the iron into plastic
   G. attract it   J. push the piece of iron away

AG 98   Assessment Guide   (page 2 of 4)   Unit E • Chapter 13

Name _____

____ 15. Which kind of magnet can be turned on and off?

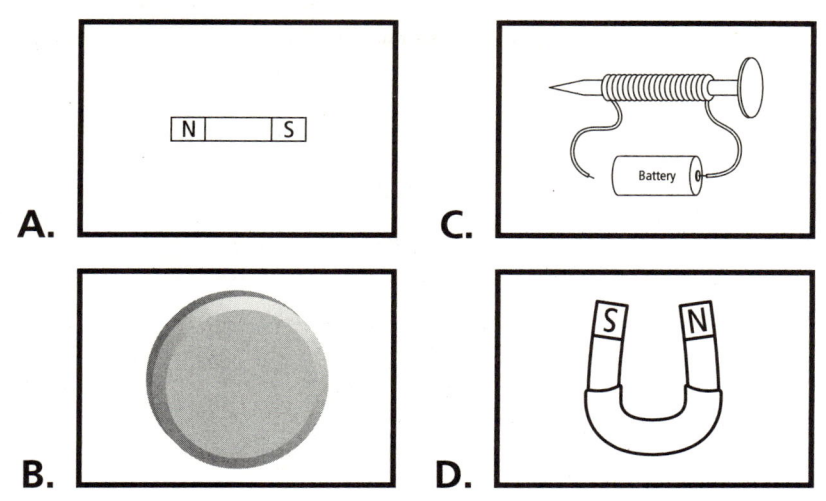

A. [bar magnet N S]

B. [circle]

C. [nail wrapped with wire connected to battery]

D. [horseshoe magnet S N]

____ 16. Samuel wanted to know why insulators are used with electric wires. Which answer would be right for you to give him?
   F. Insulation makes electricity dangerous.
   G. Insulators let electricity get out of wire.
   H. Insulators stop electricity from getting out of wire.
   J. Insulators make a path for electricity to move through.

Inquiry Skills

17. Rocco saw a crane lift a junk car from one place and then drop the car in a different place. What **hypothesis** could Rocco form about what was on the end of the crane to move the car?

   _____

18. Paul found a bag of coins in a closet. None of the coins was attracted by a magnet. What could Paul **infer** about the coins?

   _____

   _____

Unit E • Chapter 13   (page 3 of 4)   Assessment Guide   AG 99

Name _____

Critical Thinking

19. Bailey found a mixture of plastic buttons and metal safety pins in her grandmother's sewing box. She wanted to separate the buttons and the pins. What hypothesis could Bailey form about a method to quickly separate the pins from the buttons?

_____

_____

_____

20. Debbie found some magnets, but the ends of the magnets were not all marked north or south. She experimented with two of the magnets, and the results are shown in the drawing.

Identify the poles of the horseshoe magnet. Explain how you know.

_____

_____

_____

Name _____

Date _____

Performance Assessment

Student Task

Flying Paper Clip

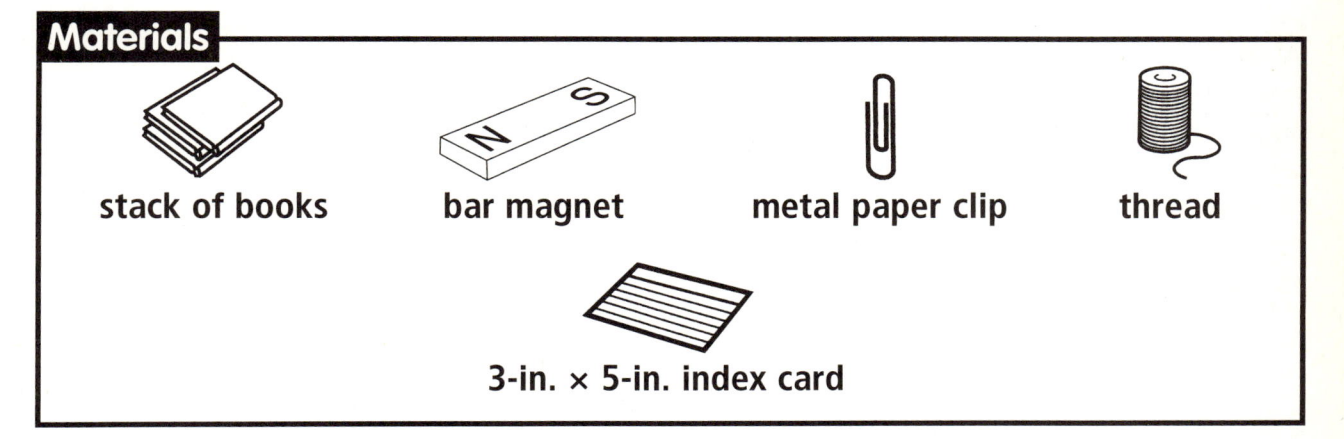

Materials

- stack of books
- bar magnet
- metal paper clip
- thread
- 3-in. × 5-in. index card

Procedure

1. Place the magnet on a stack of books so that one end extends out from the edge of the stack. Place one more book on top of the magnet to hold it in place.

2. Tie a thread to the paper clip. Tie the other end of the thread to a book, and place the book on the desk.

3. Raise the paper clip toward the magnet until the paper clip "flies."

4. While the paper clip is flying, pass the index card between the magnet and the paper clip. Observe the results.

5. Write a sentence that explains why the paper clip is held in midair.

6. Write a sentence to tell what happens when the index card is put between the magnet and the paper clip.

7. Explain what you think would happen if you used a plastic object instead of a metal paper clip.

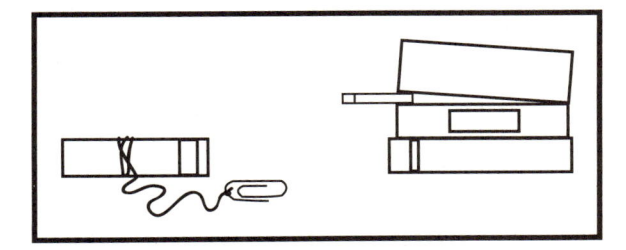

Unit E • Chapter 13

Assessment Guide   AG 101

Flying Paper Clip

Performance Assessment
Teacher's Directions

Materials Performance Task sheet, stack of books, bar magnet, metal paper clip, thread, 3-in. × 5-in. index card

Time 25 minutes

Suggested Grouping groups of two to four students

Inquiry Skills investigate, observe, draw conclusions

Preparation Hints Use metal paper clips. The thread attached to the paper clip should not be long enough to allow the paper clip to reach the magnet, yet it should be long enough to allow the paper clip to "fly." You may wish to have some plastic paper clips on hand for students who wish to test their hypotheses.

Introduce the Task Ask students to describe how a magnet can attract certain objects. Tell them they are going to show how a magnet will attract a metal paper clip and then determine whether a piece of paper will block the attraction. Model the setup for students.

Promote Discussion Ask students why the paper clip "flew." Direct the discussion toward the fact that the magnetic field was not interrupted by the index card. Ask students to hypothesize about what would have happened if a plastic object had been used instead of a metal one. Ask students if they know of any toys that use the principles they observed with the magnet and the metal paper clip.

Scoring Rubric

Performance Indicators

_____ Gathers materials quickly and works cooperatively with other team members.

_____ Follows written and oral directions to carry out the investigation.

_____ Concludes that a magnetic field is holding the paper clip in midair.

_____ Concludes that magnetic attraction is not interrupted by an index card.

Observations and Rubric Score

3	2	1	0

AG 102 Assessment Guide Unit E • Chapter 13

Name _____
Date _____

Chapter Assessment

Heat, Light, and Sound

Vocabulary

Use the terms from the box to complete the sentences.

| absorbed | conductor | insulator | opaque |
| reflection | pitch | thermal energy | shadow |

1. When light strikes an object, some of it is taken in, or _____.

2. Objects that block light are _____.

3. A dark area that forms when an object blocks the path of light is called a _____.

4. The movement of heat between objects with different temperatures is _____.

5. An object that doesn't conduct heat well is called an _____.

6. How high or low a sound is is called _____.

7. An object that heat can move through easily is called a _____.

8. The bouncing of light off an object is called _____.

Unit E • Chapter 14 (page 1 of 4) Assessment Guide AG 103

Name _____

Science Concepts

Write the letter of the best choice.

___ 9. Which of the following is a good conductor?
   A. cloth   C. plastic
   B. copper   D. wood

___ 10. Which of the following is a good insulator?
   F. aluminum   H. iron
   G. cloth   J. silver

___ 11. When can you see a reflection in a surface?
   A. when the surface is smooth and shiny
   B. when the surface is rough and uneven
   C. when the surface is black
   D. You can never see a reflection.

___ 12. What do you call a dark area that forms when an object blocks the path of light?
   F. a block   H. refraction
   G. a rainbow   J. a shadow

___ 13. When light hits an object, some of the light is reflected. What happens to the light that is not reflected?
   A. It is translucent.   C. It is absorbed.
   B. It turns white.   D. It retracts.

___ 14. Which of the following is translucent?
   F. desk   H. mirror
   G. light bulb   J. rocks

___ 15. When you talk about a sound's pitch, to what are you referring?
   A. how long or short the sound is
   B. how loud or soft the sound is
   C. how high or low the sound is
   D. the speed at which the sound travels

Name _____

___ **16.** Which of these does **not** produce vibrations?
     F. plucking strings on a harp
     G. blowing on a flute
     H. lifting a trumpet
     J. tapping on a drum

Inquiry Skills

17. Jamie went outside on a cloudy day. She hoped to see a rainbow. The sun was not out, and it had just finished raining. **Predict** whether she will see a rainbow. Explain.

_____

_____

_____

_____

18. You are wearing a shirt that reads "TOMATO" and you stand in front of a mirror. **Infer** what you will see in the mirror.

_____

_____

_____

_____

Name _____

Critical Thinking

19. Jenna is wearing a down jacket. The jacket has many air spaces. Will the jacket keep Jenna warm? Explain.

_____

_____

_____

_____

20. Look at the picture of the boats. Both people will hear the motorboat passing, but who will hear the sound more loudly? Why?

_____

_____

_____

_____

Name _____

Date _____

Performance Assessment

Student Task

Mirror Writing

Materials

2 half-sheets of paper   pen or pencil   small mirror

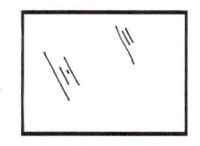

Procedure

1. Print your name on one of the sheets of paper. Place the paper face-up on your desk.

2. Stand the mirror on edge at the end of your name so that you can see your name reflected in the mirror.

3. What has happened to the letters in your name?

_____

_____

4. On the other sheet of paper, copy the way your name looks in the mirror.

5. What do you think will happen if you put the second sheet of paper next to the mirror?

_____

_____

6. Try it and see what happens.

Unit E • Chapter 14   Assessment Guide   AG 107

Mirror Writing

Performance Assessment — Teacher's Directions

Materials Performance Task sheet, 2 half-sheets of paper, pen or pencil, small mirror

Time 20–30 minutes

Suggested Grouping individuals

Inquiry Skills observe, record, communicate, draw conclusions

Preparation Hints none

Introduce the Task Begin the activity by asking students what happens to the writing on a T-shirt or a cap when you look at it in the mirror. Can you read it? Why or why not? Tell students that the great artist and inventor Leonardo da Vinci kept all of his notes in mirror writing. Ask students why they think he did that. Although no one knows for sure, many people think he did it so that people couldn't read his notebooks. Distribute the Performance Task sheets. Tell students they will make mirror writing.

Promote Discussion When students finish, have them meet in small groups to compare results. Tell students to put all of their mirror-writing sheets face down in a pile. Each student will take a sheet and will use a mirror to determine whose it is. Students can pass the names around so that everyone can view each name with a mirror. If time allows, let students write messages to each other using mirror writing.

Scoring Rubric

Performance Indicators

_____ Follows the directions for setting up the experiment.

_____ Writes his or her name using mirror writing.

_____ Predicts that the backward name will appear correctly in the mirror.

_____ Communicates and shares results in a small group, and reads other students' names and messages by using a mirror.

Observations and Rubric Score

3 2 1 0

AG 108 Assessment Guide

Unit E • Chapter 14

Name _____

Date _____

Unit Assessment

Write the letter of the best choice.

___ 1. Which property of sound shows how much energy it has?
   A. eardrum
   B. loudness
   C. pitch
   D. vibration

___ 2. Which action causes a chemical change?
   F. burning paper
   G. tearing paper
   H. drawing with a crayon on paper
   J. crumpling paper

___ 3. What does this picture show?

   A. absorption
   B. reflection
   C. refraction
   D. shadow

___ 4. Which kind of object stops thermal energy from moving between objects?
   F. conductor
   G. insulator
   H. metal
   J. thermometer

Unit E (page 1 of 6) Assessment Guide AG 109

Name _____

___ 5. Which resource is a fossil fuel?
   A. electricity
   B. oil
   C. sunlight
   D. water

___ 6. Which of these classroom objects will a magnet most likely pick up?
   F. rubber eraser
   G. plastic cup
   H. chalk
   J. metal paper clip

___ 7. What does an electromagnet use to turn a piece of metal into a magnet?
   A. electric current
   B. iron
   C. lightning
   D. wind

___ 8. What do mass, volume, and density have in common?
   F. They tell how much matter is in an object.
   G. They tell how much space an object takes up.
   H. They are physical properties of matter.
   J. They cannot be measured.

___ 9. Water boils at 100°C. Chocolate melts at about 35°C. What can you conclude from these facts?
   A. There is no relationship between temperature and heat energy.
   B. It takes the same amount of heat energy to melt chocolate as it does to boil water.
   C. It takes more heat energy to melt chocolate than to boil water.
   D. It takes more heat energy to boil water than to melt chocolate.

Name _____

___ **10.** How does light travel?
    F. in circles
    G. in curves
    H. in straight lines
    J. in a zigzag pattern

___ **11.** How will the poles of these magnets react as they move closer together?

    A. They will attract.
    B. They will repel.
    C. There will be no reaction.
    D. The magnets will stick together.

___ **12.** Which material most easily conducts current electricity?
    F. copper
    G. plastic
    H. rubber
    J. wood

___ **13.** A ball is sitting at the top of a hill. It rolls down the hill and then stops at the bottom. When does the ball have kinetic energy?
    A. before it rolls down the hill
    B. before and after it rolls down the hill
    C. as it is rolling down the hill
    D. never

Unit E   Assessment Guide

Name _____

___ 14. Which observation best demonstrates that gasoline provides energy?
   F. Gasoline can burn.
   G. Gasoline is a fossil fuel.
   H. Gasoline evaporates.
   J. Gasoline can make a car move.

___ 15. Gene uses a tank of helium to fill balloons for a party. He observes that the helium will fill a balloon of any shape or size. In which state of matter is the helium?
   A. gas
   B. liquid
   C. solid
   D. all of the above

___ 16. What kind of energy turns on the light bulb in this circuit?

   F. current electricity
   G. kinetic energy
   H. solar energy
   J. static electricity

___ 17. What happens to drinking water if enough heat is added to it?
   A. It changes from a liquid to a gas.
   B. It changes from a liquid to a solid.
   C. It changes from a solid to a liquid.
   D. It changes from a gas to a liquid.

Name _____

___ **18.** Which of the following is a solution?
    F. sand and rocks
    G. sand and water
    H. raisins baked in bread
    J. salt and water

___ **19.** What color or colors does a red T-shirt absorb?
    A. red only
    B. blue and green
    C. all colors but red
    D. all colors

Write the answer to each question.

20. Explain how you know that air is matter.

_____

_____

_____

_____

21. Compare and contrast renewable and nonrenewable resources. How are they alike? How are they different? Give examples of each kind of resource in your answer.

_____

_____

_____

_____

_____

_____

Name _____

22. Lightning is an example of static electricity. Explain why.

_____

_____

_____

23. Describe the conditions needed for a rainbow to form. Explain how a rainbow forms.

_____

_____

_____

_____

Name _____
Date _____

Chapter Assessment

Forces and Motion

Vocabulary

Match each term in Column B with its meaning in Column A.

Column A

___ 1. Force that pulls two objects toward each other

___ 2. Change of position

___ 3. Disturbance that travels through matter or space

___ 4. How far it is from one place to another

___ 5. Highest point of a wave

___ 6. Lowest part of a wave

___ 7. Distance an object moves in a certain period of time

___ 8. Any kind of push or pull

Column B

A. distance
B. trough
C. force
D. gravity
E. wave
F. speed
G. crest
H. motion

Science Concepts

Write the letter of the best choice.

___ 9. What does a ruler measure?
    A. distance   C. speed
    B. motion   D. weight

___ 10. Which surface would cause the **least** friction?
    F. dirt   H. grass
    G. ice   J. rocks

Unit F • Chapter 15   (page 1 of 4)   Assessment Guide   AG 115

Name _____

___ 11. The strength of a force and the direction of a force affect the motion of an object. What is the third thing that affects the object's motion?
    A. color   **C.** texture
    B. mass   **D.** volume

___ 12. Which object would be **most** affected by magnetic force?
    F. a marble   **H.** a paper clip
    G. a pillow   **J.** a wooden fence

___ 13. Which object would take the **least** amount of force to move?
    A. a book   **C.** a pencil
    B. a car   **D.** a table

___ 14. Look at the picture. What part of the wave is the arrow pointing to?
    F. crest
    G. disturbance
    H. trough
    J. wavelength

___ 15. There is a book on the table. You push the book to the left. At the same time, your friend pushes the book to the right. What is the net force on the book?
    A. your friend's push
    B. your push plus your friend's push
    C. your push
    D. the weight of the book

___ 16. How do scientists figure out the speed of a wave?
    F. by measuring its height
    G. by measuring its depth
    H. by measuring its wavelength
    J. by measuring the water's temperature

Name _____

Inquiry Skills

17. Look at the data below. **Interpret the data** to determine how far Runner 1 ran and how long it took her. Which runner ran the farthest?

	Distance	Direction	Time
Runner 1	1 mile	Northeast	7 min 10 sec
Runner 2	1.5 miles	South	9 min 23 sec
Runner 3	2 miles	Southwest	15 min 14 sec

_____

_____

18. Michael is going to conduct an investigation to **compare** the speed of a turtle with the speed of a rabbit. What should he use to measure their speeds? How should he conduct the investigation?

_____

_____

_____

_____

_____

Unit F • Chapter 15

Name _____

Critical Thinking

19. If friction did not exist, could you ride a bicycle? Why or why not?

_____

_____

_____

20. Jeremy and his friend are playing basketball. Describe two forces that are involved when Jeremy shoots a basketball through the net.

_____

_____

_____

_____

Name _____
Date _____

Performance Assessment

Student Task

Bobsled Races

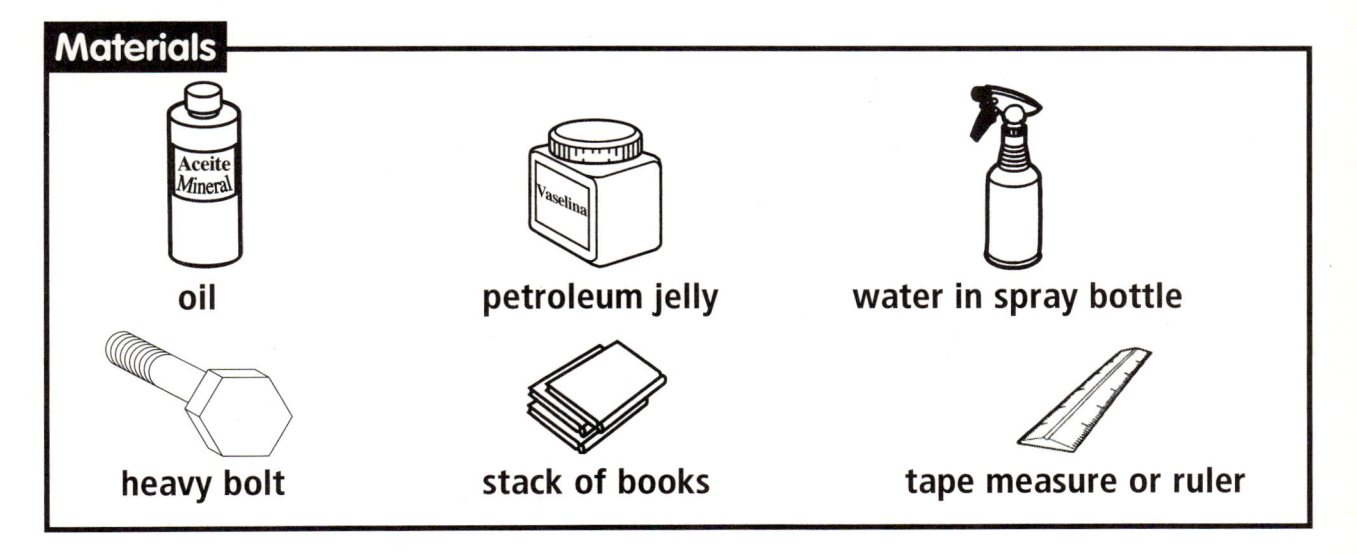

Materials

- oil
- petroleum jelly
- water in spray bottle
- heavy bolt
- stack of books
- tape measure or ruler

Procedure

Using the heavy bolt for a bobsled, compare three surfaces to find out which one allows the bolt to travel the farthest. Your teacher will provide each team with three tracks that are lined with aluminum foil.

1. Lightly cover each of the tracks with a different material (oil, petroleum jelly, or water).

2. Predict which surface will allow the bobsled to travel the farthest.

3. Test your prediction. Prop up the tracks, one at a time, on the stack of books. Give the same push to the bobsled on each track.

4. Record the distances in the data table. Was your prediction correct?

Track	Distance Traveled from Top of Ramp
Track with oil	
Track with petroleum jelly	
Track with water	

Unit F • Chapter 15   Assessment Guide   AG 119

Bobsled Races

Performance Assessment — Teacher's Directions

Materials Performance Task sheet, oil, petroleum jelly, water in spray bottle, heavy bolt, stack of books, tape measure or ruler

Time 30 minutes

Suggested Grouping groups of three or four

Inquiry Skills predict, experiment, observe, record

Preparation Hints Make three tracks for each group of students. First, cut identical strips of poster board; the strips should be about 8 cm wide and 60–90 cm long. Cover each strip with aluminum foil, folding the foil around the edges. Fold up the long sides of each strip about 2 cm to keep the bobsled from falling off. Alternatively, you may wish to have students construct the bobsled tracks. Make sure there is enough space in the room for students to conduct their trials.

Introduce the Task Begin the activity by asking students what kinds of things help reduce friction (oil, smooth ice). Then have students name things that create more friction (bumpy ice, other rough surfaces). Tell students that they will conduct an investigation to see what kind of surface allows a small, heavy object—their bolt "bobsled"—to travel the farthest.

Promote Discussion When students finish, have the groups compare results. Are they the same or different? If different, can students explain why? Were their predictions correct?

Scoring Rubric

Performance Indicators

_____ Coats each track surface with one material: oil, petroleum jelly, or water.

_____ Measures distance accurately with a tape measure or ruler.

_____ Records data in the table.

_____ Compares results to prediction.

Observations and Rubric Score

3	2	1	0

Assessment Guide — Unit F • Chapter 15

Name _____

Date _____

Chapter Assessment

Work and Machines

Vocabulary

Match each term in Column B with its meaning in Column A.

Column A

____ 1. Two inclined planes placed back to back

____ 2. A wheel with a rope around it

____ 3. The fixed point on a lever

____ 4. A simple machine that is like a nail with threads wrapped around it

____ 5. Using force to move an object

____ 6. A simple machine that makes moving and lifting things easier

____ 7. A bar that turns on a fixed point

____ 8. A machine that needs only one force to make it work

Column B

A. fulcrum
B. inclined plane
C. lever
D. pulley
E. screw
F. simple machine
G. wedge
H. work

Science Concepts

Write the letter of the best choice.

____ 9. What type of simple machine is a screwdriver?
   A. inclined plane
   B. lever
   C. pulley
   D. wheel-and-axle

____ 10. Tasha is making a poster to show pictures of levers. Which object should **not** be on her poster?
   F. nail
   G. rake
   H. broom
   J. crowbar

Unit F • Chapter 16   Assessment Guide   AG 121

Name _____

___ **11.** How is the shovel being used in this picture?
   A. as a wheel-and-axle
   B. as a wedge
   C. as an inclined plane
   D. as a lever

___ **12.** A screw is made of a post and another kind of simple machine. What is that other kind of simple machine?
   F. inclined plane
   G. pulley
   H. wedge
   J. wheel-and-axle

___ **13.** Levon's class is learning about simple machines. His teacher has written the names of four simple machines in a table on the board. As she points to each name, Levon gives an example of that machine. She writes down what he says. Which simple machine is correctly paired with its example?
   A. lever
   B. wedge
   C. pulley
   D. inclined plane

Simple Machine	Example
lever	wheelchair ramp
wedge	knife
pulley	screwdriver
inclined plane	seesaw

___ **14.** A jar lid has threads. These threads help hold the lid tightly on the jar. What simple machine is a jar lid?
   F. lever
   G. pulley
   H. screw
   J. wedge

Name _____

___ 15. Which of these is **not** an example of work?
   A. lifting a book   C. drawing with a marker
   B. opening a door   D. adding numbers in your head

___ 16. Mr. Lopez is telling his class about the human body. He describes how some athletes lift weights to make their arms stronger. An athlete holds a weight in her hand and bends her arm at the elbow. The elbow acts as a fulcrum.

In his example, the arm is a simple machine. Which machine is it?
   F. lever
   G. pulley
   H. screw
   J. wheel-and-axle

Inquiry Skills

17. Megan needs to keep a door propped open. **Predict** which simple machine Megan will choose to do the job. Explain.

_____

_____

18. **Interpret** the pictures to decide which screw is easier to turn. Explain.

_____

_____

Unit F • Chapter 16   (page 3 of 4)   Assessment Guide   AG 123

Name _____

Critical Thinking

19. The pictures show two simple machines. Tell how the machines are alike.

_____
_____
_____
_____
_____
_____

20. Luis has made two ramps. Ramp A is steeper than Ramp B. Which ramp will make it easier for Luis to move the block of wood? Tell how you know.

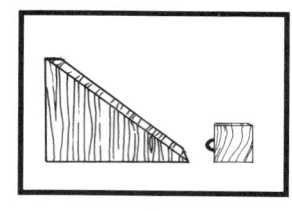

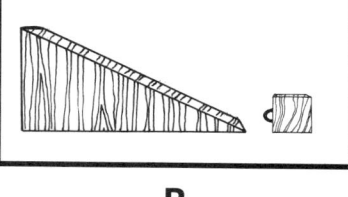

_____
_____
_____

Name _____
Date _____

Performance Assessment

Student Task

Lever and Fulcrum

Materials

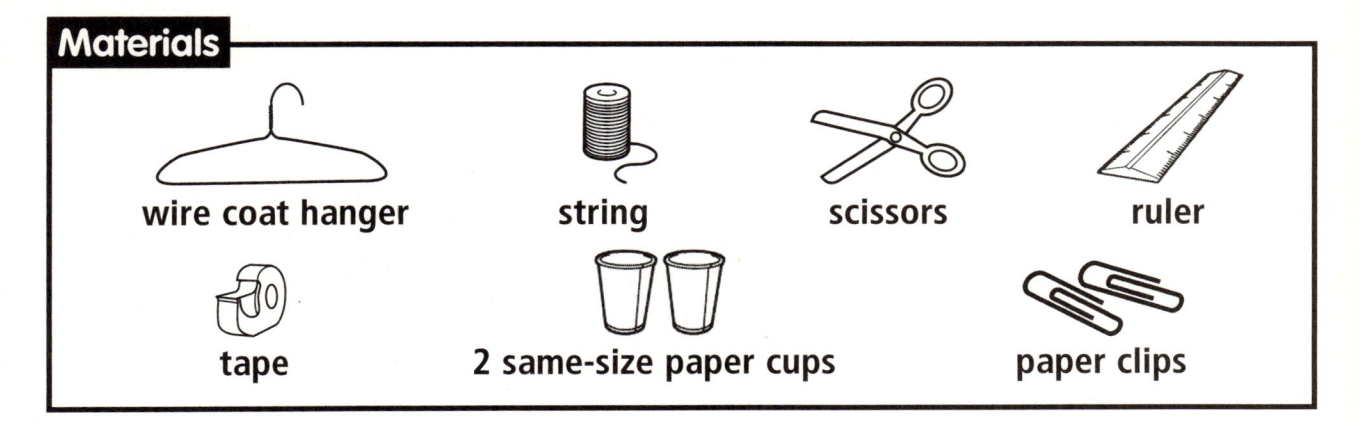

- wire coat hanger
- string
- scissors
- ruler
- tape
- 2 same-size paper cups
- paper clips

Procedure

1. Use string to hang a wire hanger by its top. The top is a fulcrum.

2. Measure to find the middle of the bottom part of the hanger. Mark the middle with a small piece of tape. This shows the position of the fulcrum on top of the hanger.

3. Label one cup L for *load* and the other cup F for *force*. Hang each cup an equal distance from the center of the hanger, as shown. Tape the strings so they don't slide.

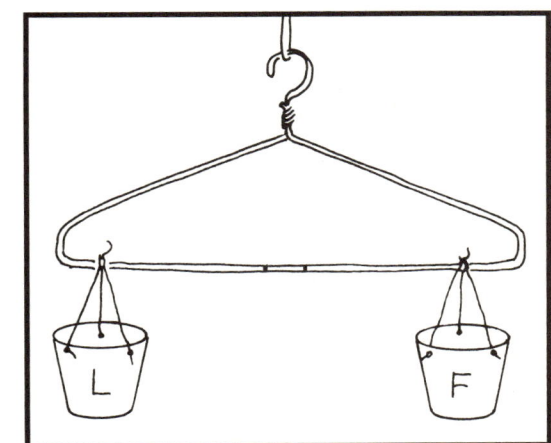

4. Put 10 paper clips in Cup L. Add paper clips one by one to Cup F until the hanger is level. Record the number of paper clips you add.

5. Move Cup L 4 cm closer to the fulcrum mark, and retape it. Then repeat Step 4. Again, record the number of paper clips you add to make the hanger level. How does the distance from the fulcrum relate to the force that lifts the load?

Unit F • Chapter 16

Assessment Guide   AG 125

Lever and Fulcrum

Performance Assessment
Teacher's Directions

Materials Performance Task sheet, wire coat hanger, string, scissors, ruler, tape, 2 same-size paper cups, paper clips

Time 30 minutes

Suggested Grouping individuals or pairs

Inquiry Skills measure, compare, make a model, draw conclusions

Preparation Hints To assist the students, you may wish to attach the strings to the hanger and cups in advance, placing them an equal distance from the fulcrum so that the hanger is level. Tape the strings so that the cups don't move on the hanger.

Introduce the Task Ask students to define *fulcrum* and *lever* and to explain how a lever works. Encourage them to give examples of fulcrums and levers. Ask if they have ever played on a seesaw. What happens when one person on a seesaw moves closer to the fulcrum? Tell students they are going to do an experiment that will help them understand and explain how the distance from the fulcrum affects the amount of force needed to lift the load. Model setting up the experiment, including creating a data table. Demonstrate the meaning of *level* in the context of the experiment.

Promote Discussion When students finish, ask them to compare results. What did they conclude from their tables? Did they use more or fewer paper clips when the load got closer to the fulcrum? Ask them to make a general statement about how the distance from the fulcrum affects the amount of force needed to lift a load.

Scoring Rubric

Performance Indicators

- _____ Constructs a model of a lever and a fulcrum to test the amount of force needed to lift a load.
- _____ Measures and records observations accurately.
- _____ Constructs a table of results.
- _____ Concludes that when the load is closer to the fulcrum, it takes less force to lift the load.

Observations and Rubric Score

| 3 | 2 | 1 | 0 |

Assessment Guide

Unit F • Chapter 16

Name _____

Date _____

Unit Assessment

Write the letter of the best choice.

___ 1. Two tug-of-war teams are pulling in opposite directions on a rope. The rope does not move. Why?
  A. There are no forces acting on the rope.
  B. The net force is zero.
  C. The rope has too much mass.
  D. Gravity is too strong.

___ 2. Which of the following is a simple machine?
  F. pillow
  G. dishwasher
  H. broom
  J. engine

___ 3. Why does it take less force to turn a screw into wood than to drive a nail into wood?
  A. Screws are shorter than nails.
  B. Screws act like levers, so they apply a greater force than nails.
  C. The threads on the screw increase the distance it travels.
  D. Screws do more work than nails.

___ 4. Which wave has the longest wavelength?

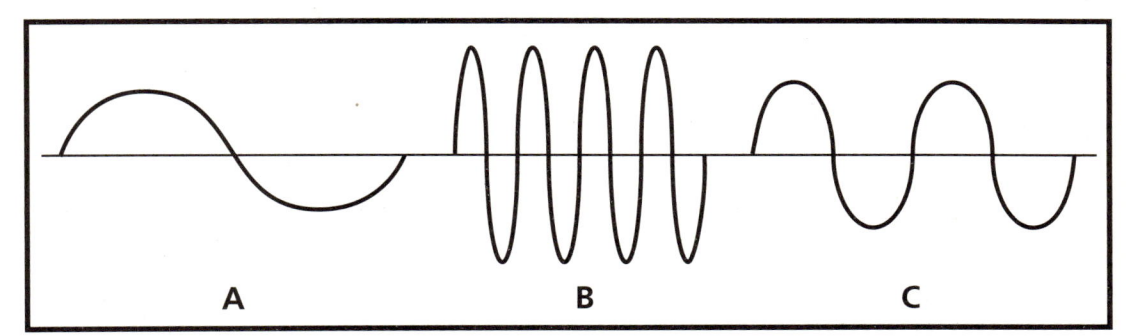

  F. Wave A
  G. Wave B
  H. Wave C
  J. There is not enough information to decide.

Unit F   (page 1 of 6)   Assessment Guide   AG 127

Name _____

___ 5. Why does the same force move a baseball farther than a bowling ball?
   A. The baseball is softer.
   B. The baseball has a rougher surface.
   C. The baseball has less volume.
   D. The baseball has less mass.

___ 6. What type of simple machine is a seesaw?

   F. lever
   G. pulley
   H. wheel-and-axle
   J. all of the above

___ 7. A dog pushes a bone across the floor. The bone moves to the left. In which direction did the dog probably push the bone?
   A. right
   B. left
   C. down
   D. up

___ 8. Which two measurements are needed to find the speed of an object?
   F. force and mass
   G. time and wavelength
   H. position and force
   J. time and distance

Name _____

___ 9. Which simple machine would best help movers put boxes in the back of a tall truck?
    A. inclined plane
    B. screw
    C. wedge
    D. wheel-and-axle

___ 10. Which activity would a scientist say involves work?
    F. watching a movie
    G. opening a door
    H. leaning against a wall
    J. thinking about homework

___ 11. What is the main purpose of a wedge?

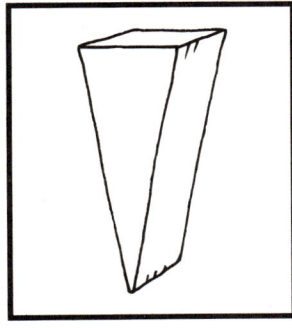

    A. to raise an object
    B. to change the direction of an object
    C. to speed up an object
    D. to split an object apart

___ 12. Why are waves able to move matter?
    F. They have speed.
    G. They have long wavelengths.
    H. They carry energy.
    J. They have weight.

Unit F   Assessment Guide

Name _____

___ 13. What type of simple machine could best be used to close curtains?
   A. inclined plane
   B. lever
   C. pulley
   D. wheel-and-axle

___ 14. Which statement about force is **false**?
   F. Forces always start objects moving.
   G. A moving object will keep moving until a force stops it.
   H. The stronger the force, the greater the change in motion.
   J. An object moves in the direction of the force pushing or pulling it.

___ 15. What is the main purpose of a machine?
   A. to change the speed of an object
   B. to change the way work is done
   C. to turn an object
   D. to eliminate work

___ 16. Tyrese pulls a chair across the floor. Which two things would he need to measure to find the amount of work he has done?
   F. distance and time
   G. time and wavelength
   H. time and force
   J. force and distance

___ 17. Which force always pulls objects toward Earth?
   A. friction
   B. gravity
   C. magnetic force
   D. net force

Name _____

___ **18.** What type of simple machine is a doorknob?

    F. lever   **H.** screw
    G. pulley   **J.** wheel-and-axle

___ **19.** Two airplanes, A and B, leave an airport at the same time. They each fly for 2 hours. Airplane A travels 800 miles. Airplane B travels 600 miles. How is this possible?
    A. Airplane A flew at a greater speed.
    B. Airplane B flew at a greater speed.
    C. Airplane A flew a shorter distance.
    D. Airplane B flew a longer time.

Write the answer to each question.

20. Suppose your job is to lift a heavy box onto a platform. Describe two different ways you could use a simple machine to move the box. Explain how each machine changes the way you do work.

_____
_____
_____
_____
_____

Name _____

21. Suppose you are playing soccer. Identify two things that affect how far you kick the ball. Describe the effects of each one.

_____
_____
_____
_____

22. Summarize the relationship between speed, distance, and time. Use speed to explain how two cars can leave at the same time and travel the same route but arrive at different times.

_____
_____
_____
_____

23. Tara pushes very hard on a box of books. No matter how hard she pushes, the box does not move. Does Tara do work? Explain.

_____
_____
_____
_____

Introduction • Getting Ready for Science

Name _____
Date _____

Chapter Assessment

Getting Ready for Science

Vocabulary — 4 points each

Match each term in Column B with its meaning in Column A.

Column A

G 1. A test done to find out whether a hypothesis is correct
E 2. The one thing in a scientific test that is different
H 3. The study that a scientist does
F 4. An organized plan that scientists use to conduct a study
C 5. A possible answer to a question
D 6. A tool used to pick up and hold on to objects
B 7. The questioning or close study of something
A 8. To come up with a plan or a model

Column B

A. formulate
B. inquiry
C. hypothesis
D. forceps
E. variable
F. scientific method
G. experiment
H. investigation

Science Concepts — 5 points each

Write the letter of the best choice.

B 9. Which tool would you use to measure the distance around the trunk of a tree?
　A. hand lens
　B. measuring tape
　C. ruler
　D. thermometer

Name _____

F 10. Which of these is **not** an inquiry skill?
　F. coloring　　H. measuring
　G. comparing　J. predicting

C 11. What would you use this tool to measure?
　A. mass of a solid
　B. weight of a solid
　C. volume of a liquid
　D. temperature of a liquid

J 12. Which is the first step in the scientific method?
　F. draw a conclusion
　G. plan an experiment
　H. form a hypothesis
　J. observe and ask questions

B 13. Suppose you use two balls of different sizes to represent Earth and the moon. What inquiry skill do you use?
　A. classify
　B. formulate models
　C. predict
　D. use time/space relationships

H 14. Miguel made a graph showing how many students have blue or brown eyes. What inquiry skill did he use?
　F. infer
　G. order
　H. display data
　J. make a prediction

Name _____

B 15. Which tool would you use to see the parts of a ladybug up close?
　A. forceps
　B. hand lens
　C. measuring tape
　D. thermometer

G 16. David is using the scientific method to study how plants grow. In one step, he identifies variables and lists the equipment he will use. What is he doing in this step?
　F. gathering data
　G. planning an experiment
　H. drawing a conclusion
　J. investigating further

C 17. Mara needs to measure a small amount of powder. Which tool should she use?
　A.　　C.
　B.　　D.

J 18. Which statement is a good hypothesis?
　F. Bubbles are round.
　G. Some bubbles are very big.
　H. Bubbles are fun to look at and play with.
　J. A flexible wand makes better bubbles than a stiff wand.

Name _____

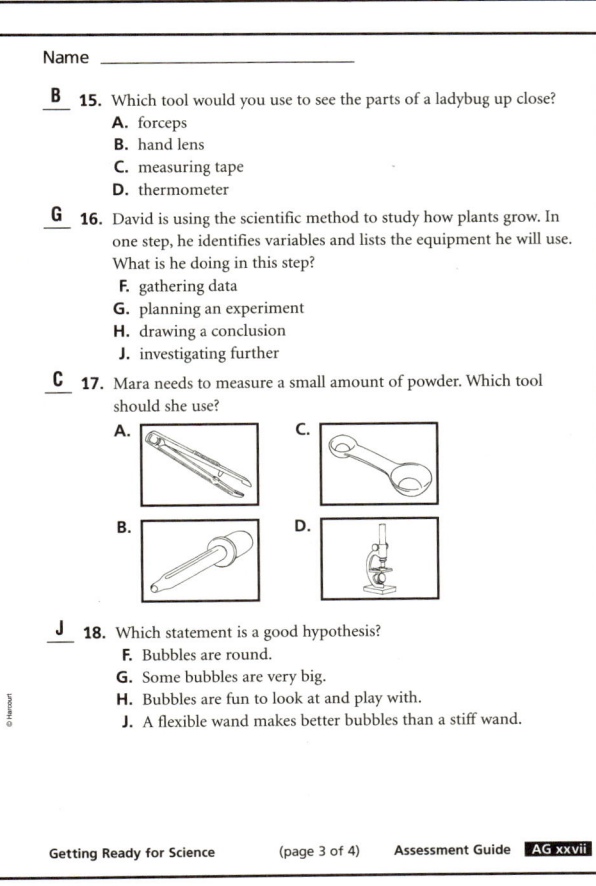

Critical Thinking — 9 points each

19. What inquiry skills are necessary for planning an experiment?
　Possible answer: You could use the following inquiry skills to plan an experiment: communicate, plan, identify and control variables, and formulate or use models.

20. You wish to investigate why some objects float and others do not. Write a hypothesis you could test. Then write a simple plan for an experiment to test your hypothesis.
　Answers will vary. Hypotheses should be reasonable and testable, and the variable to be tested should be clearly identified. Experimental plans should be simple but contain sufficient steps to test the hypothesis.

Answer Key　　　**Assessment Guide**

Unit A • Chapter 1

Name _____
Date _____

Chapter Assessment

Types of Living Things

Vocabulary 4 points each

Match each term in Column B with its meaning in Column A.

	Column A	Column B
B	1. The changes that happen to an organism during its life	A. organism
D	2. Passed on from parents	B. life cycle
E	3. A tiny building block that makes up every part of an organism	C. metamorphosis
F	4. An organism, wrapped in a chrysalis, that doesn't move or eat	D. inherited
C	5. Series of changes in appearance	E. cell
A	6. Any living thing	F. pupa

Science Concepts 4 points each

Write the letter of the best choice.

C 7. Which of the following is an example of how a living thing is different from a nonliving thing?
  A. Nonliving things reproduce.
  B. Living things don't move.
  C. Living things reproduce.
  D. Nonliving things breathe.

G 8. What do all living things use to grow?
  F. air   H. heat
  G. energy   J. skin

B 9. What type of cells keep a plant in the ground?
  A. leaf   C. skin
  B. root   D. stem

H 10. Which do you use to look at a cell?
  F. binoculars   H. microscope
  G. magnifying glass   J. thermometer

B 11. Look at the picture. What part of the cell is the arrow pointing to?
  A. chloroplast
  B. cell membrane
  C. cytoplasm
  D. vacuole

H 12. What part of the cell tells the cell how to do its job?
  F. cell membrane   H. nucleus
  G. cytoplasm   J. vacuole

B 13. What does a plant cell have that an animal cell does not have?
  A. cell membrane   C. nucleus
  B. cell wall   D. vacuole

F 14. How do tulips and daffodils begin their life cycles?
  F. bulb   H. stem
  G. seed   J. tuber

C 15. Which sequence is correct in the life cycle of an organism?
  A. birth, reproduction, growth, death
  B. birth, death, reproduction, growth
  C. birth, growth, reproduction, death
  D. growth, reproduction, birth, death

G 16. Which is an inherited trait?
  F. learning to talk
  G. having brown eyes
  H. learning to ride a bike
  J. having several hobbies

Inquiry Skills 8 points each

17. Lisa plants a seed in soil in a pot. Then she places the pot inside her bedroom closet. She waters the seed every other day for a week. **Infer** what will happen to the seed in a week. Explain.

   Possible answer: The seed will sprout because seeds do not need light to grow.

18. Megan has two dogs. One is a female and the other is a male. Both dogs have white fur and blue eyes. If the dogs have a puppy, **infer** what the puppy will look like. Explain.

   Possible answer: Since both dogs have white fur and blue eyes, the puppy will probably inherit both of those traits. The puppy will have white fur and blue eyes.

Critical Thinking 10 points each

19. A grasshopper goes through an incomplete metamorphosis. A butterfly goes through a complete metamorphosis. Use these insects to explain the difference between an incomplete metamorphosis and a complete metamorphosis.

   A grasshopper looks the same during its entire life cycle. When a grasshopper hatches from an egg, it looks like a tiny adult. At each step, the grasshopper grows bigger but looks the same. The butterfly's appearance totally changes during its life cycle. The life cycle begins when an egg hatches into a caterpillar. Then, the caterpillar wraps itself in a chrysalis. It emerges from the chrysalis as an adult butterfly.

20. Label the parts of the plant cell.
   A. **nucleus**
   B. **cell wall**
   C. **cytoplasm**
   D. **cell membrane**
   E. **chloroplast**
   F. **vacuole**

Unit A • Chapter 2

Name _____
Date _____

Chapter Assessment

Types of Plants

Vocabulary 4 points each

Match each term in Column B with its meaning in Column A.

Column A | Column B

_B_ 1. The first stage of life for many plants — A. stem
_E_ 2. The food factory in a plant — B. seed
_A_ 3. The plant part that connects the roots to the leaves — C. evergreen
_H_ 4. The substance that helps plants turn energy from the sun into food — D. root
_F_ 5. A plant that loses its leaves each year — E. leaf
_D_ 6. The part of a plant that grows underground — F. deciduous
_G_ 7. The process a plant uses to make food — G. photosynthesis
_C_ 8. A plant that makes food all year long — H. chlorophyll

Science Concepts 4 points each

Write the letter of the best choice.

_D_ 9. Which of these things does a plant need to live?
  A. fertilizer   C. warmth
  B. oxygen   D. water

_G_ 10. Plants can live almost anywhere on Earth. What is one way for a desert plant to have enough water?
  F. It loses its leaves in the winter.
  G. It stores water in a thick stem.
  H. It catches water with its leaves.
  J. It uses its water only at night.

_D_ 11. Which of these do plants need to make food?
  A. oxygen
  B. seeds
  C. soil
  D. sunlight

_F_ 12. Which is a way scientists classify plants?
  F. by leaf type
  G. by seed color
  H. by stem length
  J. by root color

_C_ 13. If a plant does not make a flower, where could it make a seed?
  A. in the stem
  B. in a root
  C. in a cone
  D. in the leaf

_J_ 14. How are all seeds alike?
  F. They are all the same color.
  G. They are all flat and pointed.
  H. They all come from spores or cones.
  J. They all look different from the plants they become.

_C_ 15. What kind of food do plants make during photosynthesis?
  A. carbon dioxide
  B. light
  C. sugar
  D. water

_F_ 16. What do plants take in during photosynthesis?
  F. carbon dioxide
  G. oxygen
  H. soil
  J. sugar

Inquiry Skills 8 points each

17. Three identical plants were planted in the same kind of soil. The first plant was watered three times every day for two weeks. The second plant was watered once every two days. The third plant was watered once a week. Scientists often **compare** the results they get in their experiments. How would you compare the plants to decide which one received the right amount of water?

   Possible answer: I would measure the plants to see which has the longest stem. I would also see which plant is greenest.

18. Two plants were planted in the same type of soil. One was placed in the closet, and one was placed on a sunny windowsill. They were given equal amounts of water for two weeks. **Predict** which plant will be healthier. Explain.

   The plant on the windowsill will be healthier. The plant in the closet won't get the light it needs.

Critical Thinking 10 points each

19. A dandelion grows from seeds. The featherlike seeds are blown away by the wind. How can a dandelion growing in the schoolyard be a parent to young dandelion plants growing miles from school?

   The wind carried the seeds to a new location miles away, where the seeds dropped to the ground and grew into new plants.

20. The pictures show two different plants. How are Plant A and Plant B alike? How are they different?

   Plant A   Plant B

   Both plants need the same things to grow: light, air, soil, and water. Both plants have chlorophyll and make their own food. Both grow from seeds. Plant A is a deciduous plant. It makes food during one part of the year. Plant B is an evergreen. It makes food all year. Plant A makes flowers, where you can find seeds to grow a new plant. Plant B has seeds in cones instead of flowers.

Answer Key

Unit A • Chapter 3

Name _____
Date _____

Chapter Assessment

Types of Animals

Vocabulary 4 points each

Match each term in Column B with its meaning in Column A.

	Column A	Column B
D	1. An animal with feathers and wings	A. oxygen
G	2. An animal with dry, scaly skin	B. vertebrate
F	3. An animal with moist skin and no scales	C. mammal
B	4. An animal that has a backbone	D. bird
A	5. A gas animals need that is found in air and water	E. fish
H	6. An animal that has no backbone	F. amphibian
E	7. An animal with gills that lives in the water	G. reptile
C	8. An animal with fur or hair that makes milk for its young	H. invertebrate

Science Concepts 4 points each

Write the letter of the best choice.

C 9. Which is something that **all** animals need?
  A. fur C. oxygen
  B. lungs D. warmth

J 10. Which animal is a reptile?
  F. bear H. monkey
  G. bird J. snake

C 11. Which is a trait of **all** birds?
  A. They can all fly.
  B. They are all born with gills.
  C. They all hatch from eggs.
  D. They all feed their young milk.

F 12. Which animals are in the same group?
  F. crocodile and snake
  G. frog and worm
  H. ladybug and shark
  J. spider and fish

B 13. Which animal has no backbone?

A.   C.
B.   D.

G 14. Which of these is **not** a trait of mammals?
  F. have hair or fur
  G. have scales
  H. feed milk to their young
  J. breathe with lungs

C 15. How are insects and spiders alike?
  A. They both have eight legs.
  B. They both are vertebrates.
  C. They both have an outer body covering.
  D. They both have two body parts.

Name _____

J 16. Josh's brother made this table to help Josh learn about animals.

Type of Animal	Trait
amphibian	has gills as an adult
bird	lives on land and under water
fish	has feathers
reptile	has skin with scales

He told Josh that only one kind of animal is correctly paired with its trait. Which kind is this?
  F. amphibian H. mammal
  G. fish J. reptile

Inquiry Skills 8 points each

17. Animals have characteristics that make them part of a group. **Compare** and **contrast** reptiles and amphibians.

   Reptiles and amphibians are both vertebrates. Reptiles have dry skin and scales. Amphibians have moist skin.

18. A scientist finds an animal's nest. The nest has pieces of eggshell and feathers. **Infer** what this animal is and how it will get from place to place. Explain.

   The animal must be a bird because it hatched from an egg and has feathers. Since most birds can fly, it will probably fly from place to place.

Name _____

Critical Thinking 10 points each

19. Circle the animal that is **most** unlike the others. Then tell why you chose this animal.

   The honeybee should be circled because it does not have a backbone as the other two animals do.

20. A friend tells you that frogs and fish belong to the same group of animals because they can both live in a pond. Do you agree or disagree? Explain.

   I disagree. Frogs are amphibians, not fish. Fish spend their entire lives in water, but frogs spend only part of their time in water. Adult frogs breathe with lungs, fish breathe with gills. Also, fish have scales, but frogs do not.

Answer Key

Unit A

Name _____
Date _____

Unit Assessment

Write the letter of the best choice. **4 points each**

__A__ 1. What is the difference between living and nonliving things?
   A. Living things reproduce.
   B. Nonliving things reproduce.
   C. Nonliving things need energy.
   D. Living things do not need energy.

__H__ 2. What kind of food do plants make?
   F. green
   G. salt
   H. sugar
   J. water

__D__ 3. Jason found a long, thin, needle-like leaf. From what type of tree did the leaf probably come?
   A. apple
   B. maple
   C. oak
   D. pine

__G__ 4. What do all animals need in order to survive?
   F. food, warmth, sun, and eggs
   G. food, water, shelter, and oxygen
   H. sun, food, warmth, and shelter
   J. water, hair, food, and air

__D__ 5. Which is **not** an ordinary way for water to leave your body?
   A. in your breath
   B. in your sweat
   C. in your urine
   D. in your blood

Unit A (page 1 of 6) Assessment Guide **AG 19**

Name _____

__H__ 6. What do all plants need in order to survive?
   F. air, light, and shade
   G. soil, roots, and weeds
   H. soil, water, air, and light
   J. water, grass, and sun

__D__ 7. What is the first stage of growth for plants?
   A. birth
   B. eggs
   C. leaves
   D. seeds or spores

__J__ 8. What body part or parts does this animal use to help it get food?

   F. its ears
   G. its feet
   H. its skin
   J. its trunk

__D__ 9. How do insects get oxygen?
   A. from the water
   B. through their antennae
   C. by breathing air through gills
   D. through tiny holes in their bodies

AG 20 Assessment Guide (page 2 of 6) Unit A

Name _____

__G__ 10. In what part of a plant is food made?
   F. flower
   G. leaf
   H. root
   J. stem

__A__ 11. Joey has an animal that has moist skin, lays eggs in water, and has lungs. Which type of vertebrate is it most likely to be?
   A. amphibian
   B. bird
   C. fish
   D. reptile

__H__ 12. What kind of shelter do beavers build?
   F. burrows
   G. dams
   H. lodges
   J. nests

__C__ 13. What do all invertebrates have in common?
   A. All have lots of legs.
   B. All have simple bodies.
   C. None have backbones.
   D. None have wings.

__H__ 14. What part of the plant is the arrow pointing to?
   F. flower
   G. leaf
   H. root
   J. stem

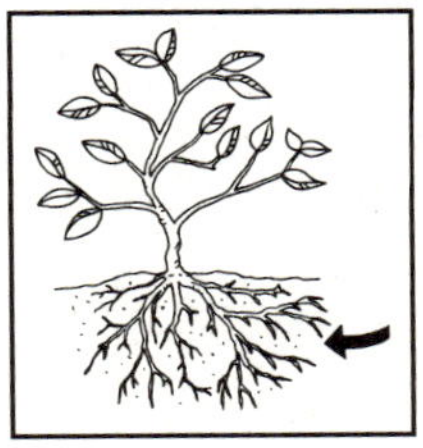

Unit A (page 3 of 6) Assessment Guide **AG 21**

Name _____

__C__ 15. To what group of vertebrates does a whale belong?
   A. amphibian
   B. fish
   C. mammal
   D. reptile

__G__ 16. What do fish use to help them breathe?
   F. fins
   G. gills
   H. scales
   J. tail

__B__ 17. Which of the following is the beginning of a life cycle?
   A. a bean
   B. birth
   C. death
   D. a root

__H__ 18. What does this picture show?

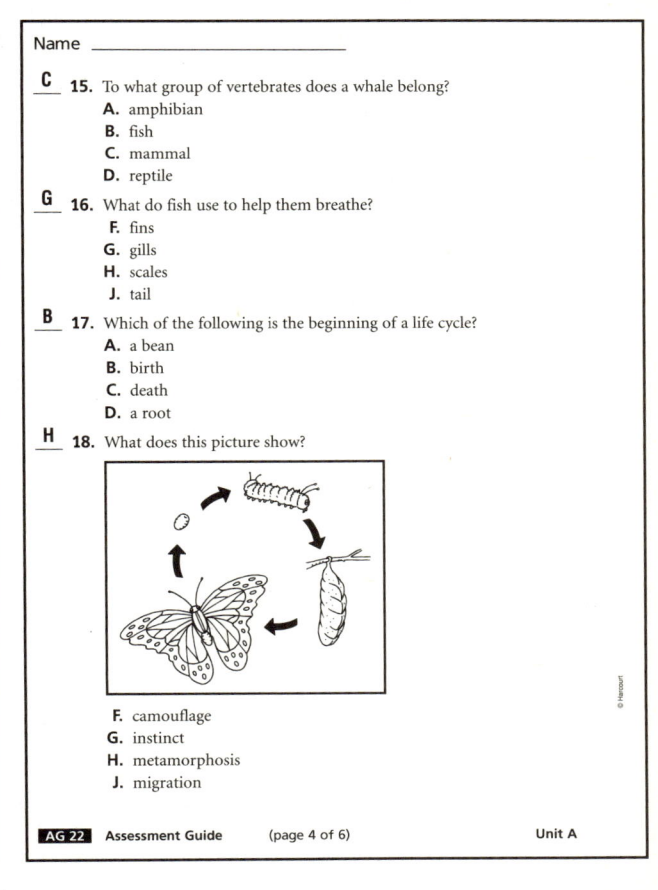

   F. camouflage
   G. instinct
   H. metamorphosis
   J. migration

AG 22 Assessment Guide (page 4 of 6) Unit A

Answer Key (page 5 of 26) Assessment Guide **AG 137**

Unit A / Unit B • Chapter 4

Name _____

__D__ 19. Which is true about insects?
  A. They all have wings.
  B. They all have four legs.
  C. They all have six body parts.
  D. There are more of them than of any other kind of animal.

Write the answer to each question. **6 points each**

20. Is this a picture of an animal cell or a plant cell? How can you tell?

   (diagram labeled "cell wall")

   Possible answer: It is a plant cell, because it has a cell wall. Animal cells do not have a cell wall.

21. Melissa planted a seed in the soil in a cave. Will the plant grow? Why or why not?

   Possible answer: The seed may sprout, but the plant will not live long without light.

Name _____

22. List three ways people use plants.
   Possible answer: People eat plants for food. They also get wood and make paper from trees. They use other plants to make cloth and medicines.

23. Grandma put earthworms in her garden. Did this help or harm her garden? Explain.
   Possible answer: This helped her garden, because earthworms improve soil. The movement of earthworms mixes air into the soil. Plants are healthier in soil that has earthworms.

Name _____
Date _____

Chapter Assessment

Where Living Things Are Found

Vocabulary 4 points each

Match each term in Column B with its meaning in Column A.

Column A
__D__ 1. A group of organisms of the same kind living in the same place
__E__ 2. Go into a sleeplike state for the winter
__G__ 3. The living and nonliving things that surround a living thing
__H__ 4. The living and nonliving things that interact in an environment
__F__ 5. Imitating the look of another animal
__C__ 6. Any trait that helps an animal survive
__A__ 7. All of the populations that live in an ecosystem at the same time
__B__ 8. The place where a population lives in an ecosystem

Column B
A. community
B. habitat
C. adaptation
D. population
E. hibernate
F. mimicry
G. environment
H. ecosystem

Science Concepts 4 points each

Write the letter of the best choice.
__D__ 9. Which of the following live in a coniferous forest?
  A. deciduous trees   C. monkeys
  B. jaguars   D. pine trees

Name _____

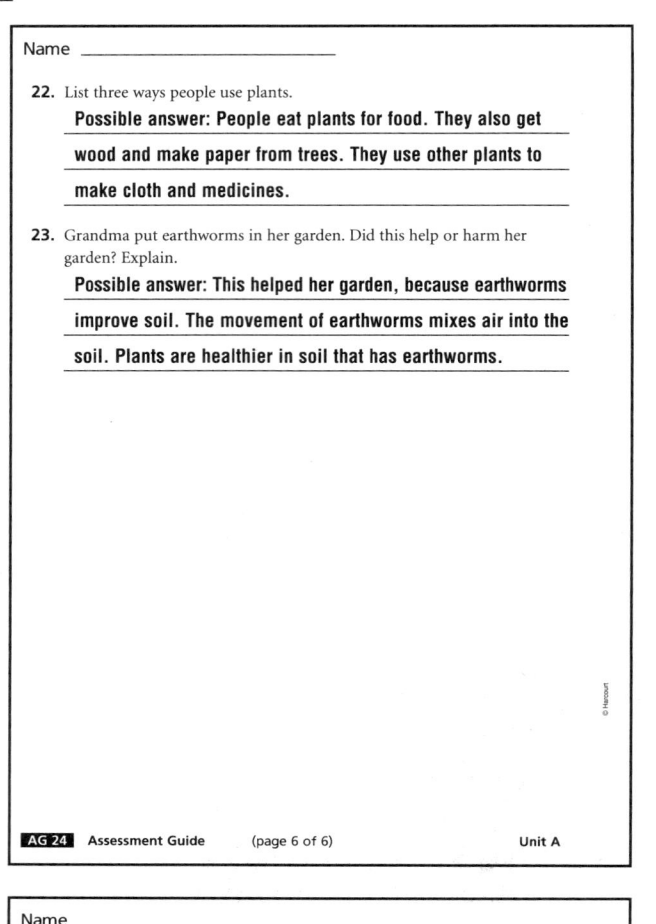

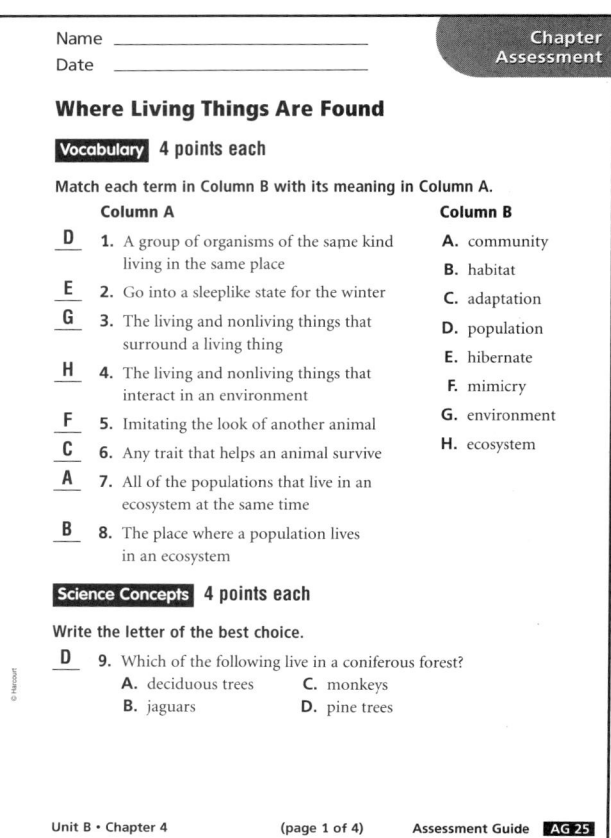

__H__ 10. In warm weather, little brown bats live in trees. When it gets cold, they move to caves, where it is warmer. What is this an example of?
  F. camouflage   H. migration
  G. hibernation J. mimicry

__A__ 11. Which is a natural event that can change an ecosystem?
  A. flooding   C. mimicry
  B. hibernation D. road building

__G__ 12. How do people help ecosystems?
  F. by building houses
  G. by planting trees
  H. by making roads
  J. by using water

__D__ 13. What kind of adaptation does the animal in the picture have?

   (picture of insect on leaf)

  A. mimicry   C. instinct
  B. hibernation D. camouflage

__J__ 14. Which is an example of an instinct?
  F. a parrot says "hello"
  G. a dolphin jumps through a hoop
  H. a dog barks on command
  J. a snake cools off in the shade

__C__ 15. Which is a nonliving part of an environment?
  A. animals   C. rocks
  B. plants   D. trees

Unit B • Chapter 4/Chapter 5

Name _____

J 16. Of which type of ecosystem is most of Earth made up?
  F. desert
  G. freshwater
  H. grassland
  J. saltwater

Inquiry Skills 8 points each

17. Devon is hiking in the Mojave Desert. **Predict** what things he might observe there. Give an example of two living and two nonliving things.
   Possible answer: Devon is in the desert, so the living things that he might see include a cactus, a snake, a lizard, and a kangaroo rat. The nonliving things are rocks and sand.

18. Compare the physical features of these two animals. What can you **infer** about how each is adapted to its environment?

   jackrabbit   arctic hare

   The arctic hare has white fur that helps camouflage it in the snow. The jackrabbit has darker fur that provides camouflage in the desert.

Unit B • Chapter 4   (page 3 of 4)   Assessment Guide   AG 27

Name _____

Critical Thinking 10 points each

19. How can damage to an ecosystem harm animals that live there?
   Possible answer: Damage may kill animals in an ecosystem, decrease their food supply, or force them to move to other ecosystems, where survival may be difficult.

20. Jason is making a poster about ecosystems. He is showing grassland, desert, coniferous forest, and saltwater ecosystems. He has the following pictures of plants and animals that he needs to place in the correct ecosystems.

   Match each plant or animal with the ecosystem that best fits its needs.
   cactus—desert; bison—grassland; dolphin—saltwater; pine tree—coniferous forest

AG 28   Assessment Guide   (page 4 of 4)   Unit B • Chapter 4

Name _____
Date _____

Chapter Assessment

Living Things Depend on One Another

Vocabulary 4 points each

Match each term in Column B with its meaning in Column A.

	Column A	Column B
E	1. A living thing that breaks down dead things for food	A. consumer
G	2. A consumer that eats only plants	B. food web
B	3. Overlapping food chains	C. carnivore
H	4. A living thing that makes its own food	D. predator
F	5. Shows the path of food from one living thing to another	E. decomposer
D	6. An animal that hunts another animal for food	F. food chain
C	7. A consumer that gets its food by eating other animals	G. herbivore
A	8. A living thing that gets energy by eating other living things as food	H. producer

Science Concepts 4 points each

Write the letter of the best choice.

B 9. Which of these is a decomposer?
  A. bee   C. grass
  B. earthworm   D. plant

F 10. Which of the following would a herbivore eat?
  F. berries   H. rabbits
  G. mice   J. worms

Unit B • Chapter 5   (page 1 of 4)   Assessment Guide   AG 31

Name _____

D 11. In which group does a grizzly bear belong?
  A. carnivore   C. herbivore
  B. decomposer   D. omnivore

G 12. Which is the producer in this simple food chain?

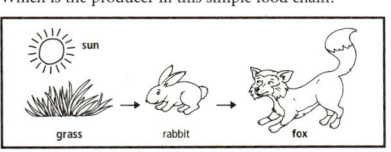

   sun   grass → rabbit → fox

  F. fox   H. rabbit
  G. grass J. sun

B 13. Hawks are predators. Which of the following is the hawk's prey?
  A. an insect   C. an octopus
  B. a mouse   D. a tiger

G 14. How might a food web change if a new plant were added?
  F. There might be fewer animals.
  G. The new plant might crowd out other plants.
  H. There might be a decrease in herbivores.
  J. There might be a decrease in carnivores.

B 15. This diagram shows how energy is used in a food chain. What is this diagram called?

  A. energy grid   C. energy chain
  B. energy pyramid D. food web

AG 32   Assessment Guide   (page 2 of 4)   Unit B • Chapter 5

Answer Key   (page 7 of 26)   Assessment Guide   AG 139

Unit B • Chapter 5/Unit B

Name _____

__F__ 16. Which is **not** an example of how prey can hide from predators?
  F. biting their own tails
  G. squirting ink and hiding behind it
  H. having a body shaped like a leaf or a stick
  J. using their own color to blend in with the environment

Inquiry Skills 8 points each

17. Sarah has these picture sorting cards. She needs to arrange the cards **to make a model** of how these things might interact in a food chain. Tell the order of these organisms in a food chain.

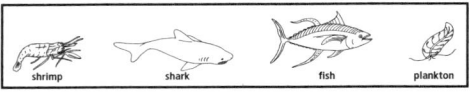

[shrimp, shark, fish, plankton]

Possible answer: The plankton is the producer and comes first on the food chain. Next comes the shrimp that would eat the plankton. Then, the large fish would eat the shrimp. Finally, the shark would eat the fish. The shrimp, fish, and shark are consumers.

18. Living things depend on one another. **Communicate** what would happen if all the producers on Earth died.
Possible answer: Plants are producers. If there were no plants to eat, animals would die and there would be no life on Earth.

Name _____

Critical Thinking 10 points each

19. Look at this food chain. What would happen if the birds became extinct?

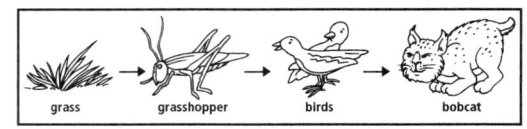

[grass → grasshopper → birds → bobcat]

Possible answer: There would probably be an increase in the grasshopper population since there would be no birds eating them. There would probably be a decrease in the bobcat population since they would lose a food source.

20. You eat several different things, so you are part of many food chains. Think about what you ate today. Tell about a food chain that includes one of the foods you ate.
Possible answer: I ate a steak, which came from a cow. The cow ate grass.

Name _____
Date _____

Unit Assessment

Write the letter of the best choice. **4 points each**

__B__ 1. What is formed by the living and nonliving things that interact in an environment?
  A. a community
  B. an ecosystem
  C. a habitat
  D. a population

__F__ 2. Which of these would be the first in a food chain?

[fox, acorn, squirrel]

  F. acorn
  G. fox
  H. squirrel
  J. fox and squirrel

__D__ 3. Which would you most likely find in an ocean?
  A. bison
  B. cactus
  C. cattails
  D. coral

__H__ 4. What do you call overlapping food chains?
  F. energy cycles
  G. energy pyramid
  H. food web
  J. producers

Name _____

__A__ 5. Which would **not** cause a change in a food web?
  A. a sunny day
  B. a decrease in plants
  C. adding a new animal
  D. an increase in plants

__J__ 6. Which are consumers?
  F. bacteria
  G. trees
  H. mushrooms
  J. tigers

__C__ 7. A cow has flat teeth. What does this tell you about cows?
  A. They are carnivores.
  B. They are producers.
  C. They are herbivores.
  D. They are decomposers.

__H__ 8. What do you call all the frogs that live in a pond?
  F. a habitat
  G. a community
  H. a population
  J. an environment

__D__ 9. Which make up Earth's largest ecosystem?
  A. deserts
  B. forests
  C. lakes
  D. oceans

__H__ 10. Wolves hunt rabbits. What are the rabbits in this situation?
  F. consumer
  G. predator
  H. prey
  J. producer

Unit B

Name _____

B 11. Which of the following is true about deserts?
   A. There is no animal life.
   B. They are dry ecosystems.
   C. The plants need lots of water.
   D. The temperature is always mild.

H 12. Which is an example of camouflage?
   F. Whales go to Alaska.
   G. A bear sleeps through the winter.
   H. A lizard blends in with a green leaf.
   J. A nonharmful snake looks like a harmful snake.

C 13. Where do pine and fir trees grow?
   A. rain forest
   B. desert
   C. coniferous forest
   D. deciduous forest

F 14. In what habitat would you most likely find this animal?

   F. forest
   G. ocean
   H. pond
   J. rain forest

Unit B   (page 3 of 6)   Assessment Guide   AG 39

Name _____

D 15. Which is the biggest group in an energy pyramid?
   A. decomposers
   B. herbivores
   C. omnivores
   D. producers

Use the picture to answer Questions 16–17.

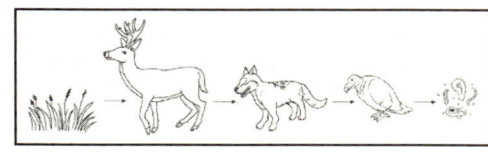

G 16. Which is the producer in this food chain?
   F. deer
   G. grass
   H. vulture
   J. wolf

A 17. Which is the decomposer in this food chain?
   A. bacteria
   B. grass
   C. vulture
   D. wolf

H 18. Which of the following includes a baby fish's knowing how to swim?
   F. adaptations
   G. hibernation
   H. instincts
   J. migration

AG 40   Assessment Guide   (page 4 of 6)   Unit B

Name _____

D 19. A chimpanzee eats fruits and insects. Which of the following terms describes the chimpanzee?
   A. carnivore
   B. decomposer
   C. herbivore
   D. omnivore

Write the answer to each question. **6 points each**

20. How can damage to an ecosystem harm animals that live there?
   Possible answer: Damage may kill living things in an ecosystem. Damage may also force living things to move to other ecosystems, and those who stay may find survival difficult.

21. If an animal has both flat and sharp teeth, what conclusion can be made about the food it eats?
   Possible answer: An animal with both sharp and flat teeth can eat both meat and plants. The animal is most likely an omnivore.

22. Explain how the loss of a forest might affect a food chain.
   Possible answer: There are many trees in a forest. Trees are producers. If the trees were gone, other parts of the food chain might die.

Unit B   (page 5 of 6)   Assessment Guide   AG 41

Name _____

23. Prey animals have ways of defending themselves against predators. These ways sometimes keep them from being caught and eaten. What effect do these ways have on a food web?
   Possible answer: A prey animal's ability to defend itself helps keep its population alive. If predators could catch and eat all prey, none of that population would be left. Then the predators might have nothing to eat and might die out.

AG 42   Assessment Guide   (page 6 of 6)   Unit B

Answer Key

Unit C • Chapter 6

Name _____
Date _____

Chapter Assessment

Minerals and Rocks

Vocabulary 4 points each

Match each term in Column B with its meaning in Column A.

	Column A	Column B
C	1. Rock that was once melted and then cooled and hardened	A. rock
F	2. Rock that has been changed by heat and pressure	B. sedimentary rock
B	3. Rock formed from material that has settled into layers	C. igneous rock
E	4. An object that is solid, formed in nature, and has never been alive	D. fossil
D	5. The remains of a living thing that died long ago	E. mineral
A	6. A naturally formed solid made of one or more minerals	F. metamorphic rock

Science Concepts 4 points each

Write the letter of the best choice.

D 7. What do you call the color of the powder left behind by a mineral when it's rubbed against a rough white tile?
 A. hematite C. rock
 B. quartz D. streak

H 8. What properties are used to identify a mineral?
 F. shape and streak H. hardness, streak, and color
 G. size and streak J. color, shape, and hardness

Name _____

B 9. What are the three layers of Earth?
 A. center, middle, outer C. core, mineral, center
 B. core, mantle, crust D. mantle, inner, outer

F 10. What type of rock is formed from volcanoes?
 F. igneous H. sandstone
 G. metamorphic J. sedimentary

C 11. What does this picture show?

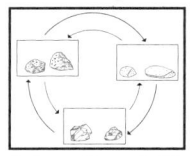

 A. how sediments build up
 B. types of soil
 C. rock cycle
 D. igneous rock

G 12. Which is an imprint fossil?
 F. bones H. shells
 G. dinosaur tracks J. teeth

B 13. What can scientists infer by finding this fossil?

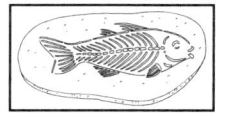

 A. the kind of food the animal ate
 B. that a sea once covered the area
 C. what animals are like today
 D. what ate this kind of animal

Name _____

H 14. Which of the following is **not** a mineral?
 F. diamond H. granite
 G. gold J. quartz

D 15. Why are plant fossils not as common as animal fossils?
 A. Plants don't have teeth.
 B. Plants are smaller than animals.
 C. There were more animals than plants.
 D. The soft parts of plants are easily destroyed.

F 16. What is formed when mud or minerals fill a mold?
 F. cast H. rock
 G. fossil J. wood

Inquiry Skills 8 points each

17. Tim needs to create a science fair project. His mother suggested that he **make and use a model** of a fossil. Tim wants to make a mold and cast a fossil. How can he do this?

 Possible answer: Tim can make an impression of a shell in clay to create the model of a mold fossil. He can fill that clay impression with glue. When the glue dries, he can pull out the dried glue to produce the cast fossil model.

Name _____

18. Knowing the hardness of a mineral can help you identify it. The Mohs scale below tells the hardness of a mineral. Use it to write the correct **order** from hardest to softest for the following minerals: topaz, fluorite, talc, calcite, diamond, and quartz.

1 Talc	2 Gypsum	3 Calcite	4 Fluorite	5 Apatite
6 Orthoclase feldspar	7 Quartz	8 Topaz	9 Corundum	10 Diamond

The correct order from hardest to softest is: diamond (10), topaz (8), quartz (7), fluorite (4), calcite (3), talc (1).

Critical Thinking 10 points each

19. Why are most fossils found in sedimentary rock?

 Most fossils are found in sedimentary rock because the remains of a living thing are sometimes buried in the particles that form sedimentary rock. Few fossils form in metamorphic and igneous rock, because the pressure and heat that form these rocks often destroy plant and animal parts before they become fossils.

20. Mrs. Smith's class has a collection of rocks. If igneous rock were kept in the classroom for six months, would it change into metamorphic rock? Why or why not?

 Possible answer: No; it would not change into metamorphic rock, because great heat and pressure are needed to change an igneous rock into a metamorphic rock. Also, it takes a long time for one kind of rock to change into another kind.

Unit C • Chapter 7

Forces That Shape the Land

Vocabulary 4 points each

Match each term in Column B with its meaning in Column A.

	Column A	Column B
D 1.	An opening on Earth's surface from which lava flows	A. earthquake
B 2.	A flat area higher than the land around it	B. plateau
F 3.	A large amount of water that covers normally dry land	C. glacier
H 4.	The movement of weathered rock and soil	D. volcano
G 5.	The way rocks are broken down into smaller pieces	E. canyon
A 6.	The shaking of Earth's surface	F. flood
E 7.	A valley with steep sides	G. weathering
C 8.	A huge block of ice	H. erosion

Science Concepts 4 points each

Write the letter of the best choice.

B 9. Which of the following does **not** cause weathering?
   A. plant roots
   B. soil
   C. water
   D. wind

F 10. Which of the following is a very slow type of erosion that moves rocks and soil?
   F. creep   H. landslide
   G. fault   J. volcano

B 11. What does this illustration show?
   A. canyon
   B. glacier
   C. plateau
   D. valley

J 12. What causes a flood?
   F. drought
   G. landslides
   H. gas and ash that erupt from a volcano
   J. heavy rainfall that makes rivers overflow

B 13. Where can you find beaches?
   A. canyon   C. Great Plains
   B. coastal plains   D. mountains

H 14. What is a butte?
   F. a deep canyon
   G. a table made of rock
   H. a flat-topped hill with steep sides
   J. a rocky mountain

D 15. Which of the following causes sand dunes?
   A. earthquakes   C. landslides
   B. rain   D. wind

G 16. Which of these causes a quick change to the land?
   F. erosion   H. weathering
   G. volcano   J. wind

Inquiry Skills 8 points each

17. **Compare** a plateau with a footstool. How are they alike?
   Possible answer: Both have flat tops and are higher than the surrounding surface.

18. Look at the two bars of the graph. **Interpret the data** to explain how the change happened.

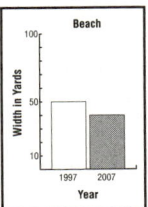

   Possible answer: The beach became smaller because the land eroded over time.

Critical Thinking 10 points each

19. Imagine you are examining an old map of a town you are visiting. The map is hundreds of years old. You notice that the river today is not where it is on the map. Is this possible? Explain.
   Yes. It is possible for a river to change its course over time. Fast-moving water carries rocks and soil and then drops them when it moves more slowly. New land builds up and changes the course of the river.

20. In which of these three areas could a landslide happen? Explain your answer.

   A desert   B mountains   C lake

   Possible answer: A landslide could happen in Picture B. Landslides are large amounts of rock or soil that slide down hills or mountains. There couldn't be a landslide on the flat land of the desert or in a lake.

Answer Key

Unit C • Chapter 8

Name _____
Date _____

Chapter Assessment

Conserving Resources

Vocabulary 4 points each

Match each term in Column B with its meaning in Column A.

Column A	Column B
_F_ 1. Saving resources by using them wisely	A. humus
_G_ 2. To use less of things	B. recycle
_E_ 3. Any harmful material in the environment	C. resource
_B_ 4. To break down or change a product and use it to make something new	D. reusable resource
_C_ 5. A material that is found in nature and is used by living things	E. pollution
_H_ 6. To use again and again	F. conservation
_D_ 7. A resource that can be used again and again	G. reduce
_A_ 8. The part of soil made up of dead plants and animals	H. reuse

Science Concepts 4 points each

Write the letter of the best choice.

_D_ 9. Which resource is found below ground?
  A. air
  B. cotton
  C. gasoline
  D. oil

Name _____

_J_ 10. Which of the following resources is renewable?
  F. coal   H. soil
  G. gasoline J. trees

_C_ 11. Which layer of soil is the arrow pointing to?
  A. bedrock
  B. clay soil
  C. subsoil
  D. topsoil

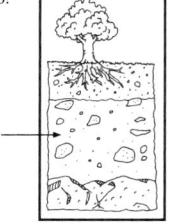

_H_ 12. What can cause pollution in the air and on land to get into water?
  F. cars   H. rain
  G. factories   J. water treatments

_D_ 13. You use the same skis that are now too small for your older brother. What are you doing?
  A. recycling resources   C. reinventing resources
  B. reducing resources   D. reusing resources

_G_ 14. Which product can be made from recycled plastic?
  F. cans   H. greeting cards
  G. doormats   J. newspaper

_D_ 15. Which is **not** mined from the land?
  A. coal   C. gold
  B. gemstones D. wood

Name _____

_H_ 16. What type of soil is made up of powdery grains of rock?
  F. humus   H. clay
  G. loam   J. sand

Inquiry Skills 8 points each

17. **Compare** the two pictures. In which place would you **infer** that people need to conserve water? Why?

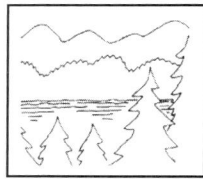

   Possible answer: People need to conserve water in the desert because there is little water there.

18. **Compare** what it means to reduce use of resources and to reuse resources. Give an example of each.

   Possible answer: To reduce use of resources means to use less of them. An example of this is using less water when taking a bath. To reuse resources means to use something again and again. An example of this is to fix broken toys instead of buying new ones.

Name _____

Critical Thinking 10 points each

19. Karen learned that water is a reusable resource. She was told that water used to wash dishes or clothes can be reused. The thought of reusing that water did not seem like a good idea to her. What makes it possible to reuse this water? Explain your answer.

   Possible answer: When you drain the used water it goes to a water treatment plant. There, all the chemicals and dirt are removed so that the water can be reused.

20. Frances wants to grow tomatoes. The area that she chose for her tomato plants has clay soil. Why would this area not be good for growing tomatoes? If she must plant the tomatoes there, what can she do to prepare the soil?

   Possible answer: The clay soil may be too hard or too wet for the tomato seeds. If Frances needs to plant there, she can mix some silt, sand, and humus into the soil to make loam, which is the best type of soil for growing vegetables.

Unit C

Name _____
Date _____

Unit Assessment

Write the letter of the best choice. **4 points each**

__D__ 1. Which is **not** a property of a mineral?
   A. color
   B. hardness
   C. streak
   D. temperature

__G__ 2. Which is a way to cut down on pollution?
   F. drive cars
   G. walk to school
   H. dump oil in the ocean
   J. throw trash on the street

__B__ 3. Which is a nonrenewable resource?
   A. animals
   B. soil
   C. trees
   D. water

__G__ 4. What are Earth's highest landforms?
   F. canyons
   G. mountains
   H. plains
   J. valleys

__B__ 5. What are the three main layers of Earth?
   A. center, crust, mantle
   B. crust, mantle, core
   C. crust, middle, outer
   D. mantle, inner, outer

Unit C   (page 1 of 6)   Assessment Guide   AG 61

Name _____

__H__ 6. What type of landform is found in the middle of the United States?
   F. beaches
   G. glaciers
   H. plains
   J. valleys

__D__ 7. What four things make up soil?
   A. water, sand, dirt, and seeds
   B. fossils, humus, water, and dirt
   C. air, grain, dirt, and tiny pieces of rock
   D. water, air, humus, and tiny pieces of rock

__F__ 8. What is the process that moves pieces of rock and soil?
   F. erosion
   G. delta
   H. mudslide
   J. weathering

__C__ 9. In which of the following would you be most likely to find a fossil?
   A. lava rock
   B. igneous rock
   C. sedimentary rock
   D. metamorphic rock

__G__ 10. What is formed when mud or minerals fill a mold?
   F. bone
   G. cast
   H. rock
   J. soil

AG 62   Assessment Guide   (page 2 of 6)   Unit C

Name _____

__A__ 11. Rock that melts, cools, and hardens becomes what type of rock?
   A. igneous
   B. marble
   C. metamorphic
   D. sedimentary

__F__ 12. Which of the following can help clean the air?
   F. plants, wind, and rain
   G. cars, gasoline, and rain
   H. trees, factories, and plants
   J. cars, exhaust, and factories

__D__ 13. What causes erosion?
   A. heat
   B. cold
   C. sun and water
   D. wind or water

__J__ 14. Which of these is an effect of an earthquake?
   F. areas covered with lava
   G. gas clouds
   H. burned forests
   J. uneven areas of ground

__C__ 15. What type of soil is primarily found on farms?
   A. clay
   B. dirt
   C. loam
   D. rocks

Unit C   (page 3 of 6)   Assessment Guide   AG 63

Name _____

__G__ 16. What type of fossil does this picture show?

   F. cast
   G. imprint
   H. mold
   J. plant

__D__ 17. What do you call an opening on Earth's surface from which hot, melted rock flows?
   A. ash
   B. crust
   C. soil
   D. volcano

__G__ 18. What type of resource is a plant?
   F. reusable resource
   G. renewable resource
   H. refundable resource
   J. nonrenewable resource

AG 64   Assessment Guide   (page 4 of 6)   Unit C

Answer Key   (page 13 of 26)   **Assessment Guide**   AG 145

Unit C / Unit D • Chapter 9

D 19. Which lists the soils in order from biggest to smallest grains?
  A. clay, sand, silt
  B. clay, silt, sand
  C. sand, clay, silt
  D. sand, silt, clay

Write the answer to each question. **6 points each**

20. How do floods help farmers?
  Possible answer: Floods sweep over the land. They can cause a lot of damage, but the flooded rivers carry soil. When the flood waters go down, soil is left behind. This soil is rich. Farmers can grow crops in this soil.

21. Why do few fossils form in metamorphic and igneous rock?
  Possible answer: The pressure and heat that form these rocks often destroy plant and animal parts before they can become fossils.

22. Why is it important to protect renewable resources such as air and water?
  Possible answer: Even though renewable resources will always be on Earth, they can be polluted. People need clean air to breathe and clean water to drink.

23. Does weathering occur in areas that have freezing temperatures? How do you know?
  Possible answer: Yes. Water flows into cracks in rocks and then freezes. As it freezes, it takes up more space and breaks the rocks into pieces.

The Water Cycle

Vocabulary 4 points each

Match each term in Column B with its meaning in Column A.

	Column A	Column B
F	1. Rain, snow, sleet, or hail	A. fresh water
H	2. The air around Earth	B. glacier
C	3. Earth's underground supply of water	C. groundwater
D	4. The change of a gas into a liquid	D. condensation
A	5. Water that has very little salt in it	E. evaporation
G	6. The movement of water from Earth's land and water into the air and back again	F. precipitation
E	7. The change of a liquid into a gas	G. water cycle
B	8. A huge sheet of ice	H. atmosphere

Science Concepts 4 points each

Write the letter of the best choice.

B 9. Cheryl's mom is getting ready to cook pasta. When the water boils, which process will occur?
  A. condensation C. melting
  B. evaporation   D. precipitation

J 10. A radio announcer tells you it's a sunny day and the temperature is 70° F. What is the announcer describing?
  F. the atmosphere H. the water cycle
  G. the ocean   J. the weather

A 11. Trevor sees white, wispy clouds high in the sky. Which type of cloud is Trevor seeing?
  A. cirrus   C. rain
  B. cumulus D. stratus

J 12. Why is groundwater important?
  F. Groundwater warms the land.
  G. People can find groundwater easily.
  H. Groundwater contains more salt than ocean water.
  J. People use groundwater for drinking and bathing.

C 13. Luis is observing ice cubes as they change. He drew this picture. What does the picture show?
  A. boiling   C. melting
  B. freezing D. precipitation

F 14. Water moves from the air to the land, through rivers to the ocean, and back to the air. How does water move from the air to the land?
  F. It falls as precipitation.
  G. It forms as groundwater.
  H. It evaporates from the sky.
  J. It forms glaciers in Antarctica.

D 15. Which of these processes forms clouds?
  A. Water vapor expands as it rises.
  B. Solid water evaporates.
  C. Liquid water freezes.
  D. Water vapor rises and condenses.

F 16. What does an anemometer measure?
  F. wind speed   H. cloud height
  G. temperature   J. rainfall amount

Unit D • Chapter 9/Chapter 10

Name _____

Inquiry Skills 8 points each

Lindsay collected weather data for three days. She recorded the data in a table. Use the table to answer Questions 17–18.

Data	Day 1	Day 2	Day 3
Temperature	85°F	82°F	75°F
Precipitation	None	None	Rain

17. **Infer** why the temperature was cooler on Day 3.

    Possible answers: It was cooler because it rained. The sun didn't shine to warm the air as much.

18. Suppose Lindsay had also wanted to **record** the types of clouds she saw. What type of cloud would Lindsay have recorded on Day 3? Why?

    Lindsay would have recorded stratus clouds. It was raining on Day 3.

Unit D • Chapter 9   (page 3 of 4)   Assessment Guide   AG 69

Name _____

Critical Thinking 10 points each

19. Why do scientists measure precipitation?

    Scientists measure precipitation to keep records that show patterns. They use the patterns to help predict weather.

20. At 8 A.M., snow covers the ground and icicles hang from gutters. At 1 P.M., the snow is melting and the icicles are dripping. What must have happened to the temperature during these five hours? Explain.

    The temperature must have been below 0°C (32°F) at 8 A.M. because the snow and icicles weren't melting. By 1 P.M., the temperature must have risen above the freezing point of 0°C (32°F) because the snow and ice were changing from a solid to a liquid.

AG 70   Assessment Guide   (page 4 of 4)   Unit D • Chapter 9

Name _____
Date _____

Chapter Assessment

Earth's Place in the Solar System

Vocabulary 4 points each

Match each term in Column B with its meaning in Column A.

	Column A	Column B
B	1. The imaginary line Earth rotates around	A. constellation
C	2. Pattern of phases of the moon	B. axis
G	3. The sun and the planets and other objects circling it	C. lunar cycle
		D. star
H	4. A time when the moon's shadow falls on Earth	E. planet
E	5. A large body of rock or gases that revolves around the sun	F. revolution
		G. solar system
A	6. A group of stars that form a picture	H. solar eclipse
D	7. A hot ball of glowing gases	
F	8. The movement of a planet around the sun	

Science Concepts 4 points each

Write the letter of the best choice.

D 9. Light rays from the sun heat Earth. Which kind of light rays causes Earth to get the warmest?
   A. bent light rays   C. slanted light rays
   B. curved light rays   D. straight light rays

J 10. Which of these is at the center of the solar system?
   F. Earth   H. planet
   G. moon   J. sun

Unit D • Chapter 10   (page 1 of 4)   Assessment Guide   AG 73

Name _____

D 11. Which picture above shows the season when the rays from the sun are striking Earth at the greatest slant?
   A. A   C. C
   B. B   D. D

G 12. Which is **not** true of the inner planets?
   F. The inner planets have rocky surfaces.
   G. The inner planets are made mostly of gases.
   H. The inner planets are warmer than the outer planets.
   J. The inner planets are smaller than the outer planets.

B 13. In which way are Earth and Mars alike?
   A. Both planets have a watery surface.
   B. The length of a day is about the same.
   C. The distance across is about the same.
   D. The length of a year is about the same.

G 14. About how long is the lunar cycle?
   F. 7 days   H. 35 days
   G. 29 days   J. 365 days

A 15. Which is an inner planet?
   A. Earth   C. Saturn
   B. Jupiter   D. Neptune

AG 74   Assessment Guide   (page 2 of 4)   Unit D • Chapter 10

Answer Key   (page 15 of 26)   **Assessment Guide**   AG 147

Unit D • Chapter 10/Unit D

Name _____

__J__ 16. What causes a lunar eclipse?
  F. The moon changes from new moon to full moon.
  G. The sun blocks moonlight from reaching Earth.
  H. The moon blocks sunlight from reaching Earth.
  J. The Earth blocks sunlight from reaching the moon.

Inquiry Skills 8 points each

17. Ivan found a table that showed the size across of some planets in kilometers. Based on this table, in which **order** should Ivan place the planets so that they are arranged from smallest to largest?

Planet	Size
Mercury	4,800 km
Venus	12,100 km
Earth	12,800 km
Mars	6,800 km

Mercury, Mars, Venus, Earth

18. Olivia found a **model** of Earth and the sun. Based on this **model**, which seasons in North America are shown by positions A, B, C, and D?

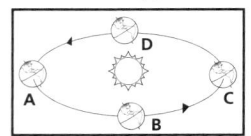

A: winter; B: spring; C: summer; D: autumn

Unit D • Chapter 10   (page 3 of 4)   Assessment Guide   AG 75

Name _____

Critical Thinking 10 points each

19. It takes Earth 365 days to revolve around the sun. If Earth revolved around the sun once every 730 days, what would happen to the length of each season?
It would double in length.

20. You have found the following diagram of the solar system. Based on this diagram, is it possible that any objects could run into each other if they keep moving in their orbits? Explain.

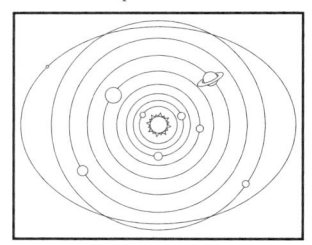

Possible answer: Yes. The orbits of the two outer objects cross, so these objects could run into each other. It looks as if other planets might also collide, because their orbits come close together.

AG 76   Assessment Guide   (page 4 of 4)   Unit D • Chapter 10

Name _____
Date _____

Unit Assessment

Write the letter of the best choice. 4 points each

__B__ 1. What is the path in which a planet revolves?
  A. a galaxy
  B. an orbit
  C. a revolution
  D. a solar system

__J__ 2. What happens to water in a pot if the water is left to boil for a long time?
  F. The water level rises.
  G. The water gets cooler.
  H. The water changes from a solid to a gas.
  J. The water changes from a liquid to a gas.

__A__ 3. What instrument would a meteorologist use to measure wind speed?
  A. anemometer
  B. map
  C. satellite
  D. thermometer

__F__ 4. In which of the following can salt water be found in all three places?
  F. oceans, gulfs, and seas
  G. ponds, lakes, and rivers
  H. gulfs, streams, and rivers
  J. streams, ponds, and oceans

__B__ 5. About how long does it take Earth to revolve around the sun?
  A. 365 hours
  B. 365 days
  C. 36 days
  D. 1 day

Unit D   (page 1 of 6)   Assessment Guide   AG 79

Name _____

__F__ 6. Which form is water in when it is water vapor?
  F. gas
  G. heat
  H. liquid
  J. solid

__D__ 7. Which of the following can be used to predict weather?
  A. map
  B. microscope
  C. rain gauge
  D. weather satellite

__H__ 8. What is the spinning of Earth on its axis?
  F. poles
  G. revolution
  H. rotation
  J. tilt

__B__ 9. Which moon phase is shown?

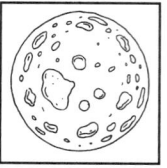

  A. first quarter   C. new moon
  B. full moon   D. third quarter

__G__ 10. Where is almost all of the fresh water on Earth found?
  F. Africa
  G. Antarctica
  H. Asia
  J. Europe

AG 80   Assessment Guide   (page 2 of 6)   Unit D

AG 148   Assessment Guide   (page 16 of 26)   Answer Key

Unit D

Name _____

B 11. The state that water is in depends on which of the following?
  A. clouds
  B. temperature
  C. vapor
  D. volume

H 12. What type of cloud is shown?

  F. circular
  G. cirrus
  H. cumulus
  J. stratus

D 13. What happens when light rays strike at a slant?
  A. The day ends.
  B. There is no light.
  C. The light is brighter.
  D. The light rays spread out more.

F 14. By which process are clouds formed?
  F. condensation
  G. evaporation
  H. melting
  J. precipitation

Name _____

D 15. What happens during a lunar eclipse?
  A. Earth blocks light from reaching the sun.
  B. The moon blocks light from reaching Earth.
  C. The moon blocks light from reaching the sun.
  D. Earth blocks light from reaching the moon.

G 16. What type of water is only a small part of the water on Earth?
  F. clear
  G. fresh
  H. salt
  J. sea

D 17. When it is summer, what can you infer about the sun's rays?
  A. They are weak.
  B. There are none.
  C. They are at a slant.
  D. They are striking directly.

J 18. What does this picture show?

  F. glacier
  G. groundwater
  H. seasons
  J. water cycle

Name _____

A 19. How long does it take Earth to rotate once?
  A. one day
  B. one month
  C. one year
  D. one hour

Write the answer to each question. 6 points each

20. Compare the inner planets to the outer planets. How are they alike? How are they different?

    Possible answer: The inner and outer planets are alike in that all orbit the sun. The inner planets have rocky surfaces and are close to the sun, warm and small. The outer planets are farther from the sun, have surfaces made mostly of frozen gases, and are colder. Most also are larger and have more moons than the inner planets.

21. If there were no water on Earth, there also would be no snow. Explain this statement.

    Possible answer: Snow is a type of precipitation. Precipitation is part of the water cycle. When the water in clouds gets heavy, it falls to Earth as precipitation. If there were no water, the water cycle would not exist.

Name _____

22. Raymond has a small red ball, a medium-size blue ball, and a desk lamp. What should he do with the materials to model a lunar eclipse?

    Possible answer: He should hold the blue ball in front of the lamp and pass the red ball behind the blue one.

23. How can predicting the chance and amount of rainfall be helpful to people?

    Possible answer: Rain is needed to grow crops, but too much of it can cause flooding. Flooding can damage homes. People can prepare if they know how much rain is predicted and how likely it is.

Answer Key

Unit E • Chapter 11

Name _____
Date _____

Chapter Assessment

Properties of Matter

Vocabulary 4 points each

Match each term in Column B with its meaning in Column A.

	Column A	Column B
E	1. The amount of matter in something	A. density
D	2. Matter with a volume and shape that stay the same	B. gas
A	3. The mass of matter compared to its volume	C. matter
G	4. A mixture in which different kinds of matter mix evenly	D. solid
B	5. Matter with no definite shape or volume	E. mass
C	6. Anything that takes up space	F. liquid
H	7. The amount of space matter takes up	G. solution
F	8. Matter with a volume that stays the same but a shape that changes	H. volume

Science Concepts 4 points each

Write the letter of the best choice.

A 9. Which of the following is matter that you cannot see?
  A. air
  B. clouds
  C. ice
  D. water

F 10. Kevin needs to measure the mass of an apple. What tool can he use?
  F. a balance   H. a ruler
  G. a barometer   J. a thermometer

C 11. Which group of words names physical properties of matter?
  A. mirror, wool, cotton   C. sour, green, hot
  B. salt, candy, sugar   D. tall, building, glass

H 12. Which of the following groups names three states of matter?
  F. gas, oil, water   H. solid, liquid, gas
  G. liquid, water, ice   J. solid, penny, liquid

D 13. Which of the following has the greatest density?
  A. cotton balls   C. jelly beans
  B. feathers   D. rocks

H 14. Mica makes a salad of oranges, apples, and bananas. What is the bowl of fruit salad an example of?
  F. condensation   H. a mixture
  G. evaporation   J. a solution

A 15. Which is a chemical change?
  A. burning wood   C. folding paper
  B. cutting cloth   D. mixing salt and water

J 16. Which of these is a solution?
  F. cereal and milk   H. orange and apple slices
  G. ice cream and nuts   J. sugar and water

Inquiry Skills 8 points each

17. Janet knows the mass of some peanuts and the mass of some pretzels. She mixes them together to make trail mix. How can she determine the mass of the trail mix if she doesn't have a tool to **measure** it? Explain.

   Possible answer: She can add the mass of the peanuts and the mass of the pretzels to find the mass of the trail mix. The mass of two or more things together is the sum of their separate masses.

18. Charlie is testing whether things sink or float. He puts a plastic-foam board in the water. **Predict** whether the board will sink or float. Explain your reasoning.

   The plastic-foam board will float, because plastic-foam is not very dense. An object that is less dense than water will float.

Critical Thinking 10 points each

19. Tyrell had a large bowl of ice cubes. He left the bowl out in the hot sun for a couple of hours. What happened to the ice cubes? Explain.

   The heat from the sun melted the solid ice cubes, causing them to change to liquid water.

20. Teresa popped some popcorn and cooked some rice. She measured a cup of each as shown in the pictures.

   Compare the volumes of the popcorn and the rice. Then determine which is denser, the popcorn or the rice. Explain.

   The volumes are the same, because volume is the amount of space that matter takes up. Both volumes fill one cup. A cup of rice has a greater mass than a cup of popped popcorn, which is mostly air. The rice is denser, because density is the mass of matter compared to its volume.

Answer Key

Unit E • Chapter 12

Name _____
Date _____

Chapter Assessment

Energy

Vocabulary 4 points each

Match each term in Column B with its meaning in Column A.

	Column A	Column B
E	1. Resource that can be replaced	A. energy
C	2. Another word for *burning*	B. resource
A	3. The ability to make something move or change	C. combustion
H	4. The energy of position	D. fossil fuels
G	5. Resource that cannot be replaced	E. renewable resource
B	6. Something in nature that people use	F. kinetic energy
F	7. The energy of motion	G. nonrenewable resource
D	8. Coal, oil, and gas	H. potential energy

Science Concepts 4 points each

Write the letter of the best choice.

D 9. Where does most of Earth's energy come from?
    A. electricity
    B. fossil fuels
    C. the moon
    D. the sun

G 10. What type of energy does a moving car have?
    F. electrical energy   H. light energy
    G. kinetic energy   J. potential energy

A 11. Which of the following is a way to save energy resources?
    A. Use a blanket instead of turning on the heater.
    B. Keep the house cool by turning on the air conditioning.
    C. Turn on the lights during the day.
    D. Leave the light on when you exit a room.

F 12. Which of the following are fossil fuels?
    F. coal and natural gas   H. light and oil
    G. water and coal   J. heat and natural gas

D 13. Which resource is renewable?
    A. coal   C. oil
    B. gas   D. wind

G 14. Which ball has **no** kinetic energy?

    F. ball 1   H. ball 3
    G. ball 2   J. ball 4

C 15. What kind of energy do plants need to grow?
    A. chemical   C. light
    B. electrical   D. sound

F 16. What tool measures wind energy?
    F. anemometer   H. sound meter
    G. light meter   J. thermometer

Inquiry Skills 8 points each

17. Tyler and his sister went to the beach. Tyler sat in the sun, and his sister sat in the shade. **Infer** what happened to each person's skin temperature. Explain.

    Possible answer: Tyler's skin temperature increased, but his sister's did not. Tyler received more heat energy from sunlight.

18. In Molly's town everyone drives a car to go anywhere. People leave their appliances on all the time, use their heaters or air conditioners every day, and do not recycle materials. **Infer** what will happen to the world if everyone acts the way people do in Molly's town.

    Possible answer: Using so much energy will cause the world to run out of fossil fuels, which are not renewable.

Critical Thinking 10 points each

19. List five ways that you can conserve energy at home or at school.

    Possible answer: I can turn off the lights when I leave a room. I can turn off the water while I brush my teeth. I can recycle paper at home and school. I can use a blanket instead of turning on the heater. I can open the blinds and curtains during the day instead of turning on the lights.

20. Carly is sitting at the top of the slide.

What type of energy does she have? Is it possible for her to change her energy? If she changes her energy, what type of energy will it become? Explain your answers.

    She has potential energy because she is just sitting at the top of the slide. Potential energy is the energy of position. If she slides down the slide, she can change her energy from potential energy into kinetic energy. Kinetic energy is the energy of motion.

Answer Key

Unit E • Chapter 13

Name _____
Date _____

Chapter Assessment

Electricity and Magnets

Vocabulary 4 points each

Match each term in Column B with its meaning in Column A.

	Column A	Column B
B 1.	An electric charge that builds up in an object	A. circuit
A 2.	A path that electricity follows	B. static electricity
D 3.	Able to attract objects made of iron	C. generator
C 4.	A machine that uses a magnet to make a current of electricity	D. magnetic

Science Concepts 4 points each

Write the letter of the best choice.

D 5. Which is an example of electricity?
  A. brush   C. hair
  B. cloud   D. lightning

F 6. What kind of electricity moves through a wire?
  F. current   H. socket
  G. motor   J. static

A 7. Which material is a good conductor of electricity for your toaster cord?
  A. copper   C. plastic
  B. insulator D. wood

F 8. What makes a refrigerator's motor do work to keep food cold?
  F. current electricity H. lightning
  G. insulator   J. static electricity

Name _____

D 9. The graph at the right shows the number of nails four different magnets are able to lift. Which magnet is the strongest?
  A. Magnet I
  B. Magnet II
  C. Magnet III
  D. Magnet IV

H 10. What are the ends of magnets called?
  F. attractors H. poles
  G. north   J. south

C 11. What is needed to make electricity?
  A. magnet only   C. both a magnet and a coil of wire
  B. coil of wire only   D. neither a magnet nor a coil of wire

H 12. Which diagram shows magnets attracting each other?
  F. 1   H. 3
  G. 2   J. 4

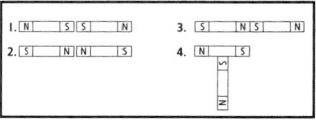

D 13. Which is **not** a use for magnets?
  A. to make electicity   C. to sort metal for recycling
  B. to make compasses   D. to separate glass from plastic

G 14. What can magnets do to a piece of iron?
  F. repel it   H. turn the iron into plastic
  G. attract it   J. push the piece of iron away

Name _____

C 15. Which kind of magnet can be turned on and off?

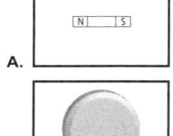

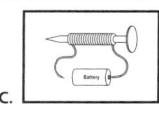

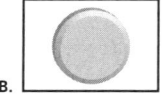

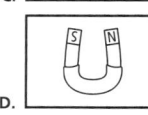

H 16. Samuel wanted to know why insulators are used with electric wires. Which answer would be right for you to give him?
  F. Insulation makes electricity dangerous.
  G. Insulators let electricity get out of wire.
  H. Insulators stop electricity from getting out of wire.
  J. Insulators make a path for electricity to move through.

Inquiry Skills 8 points each

17. Rocco saw a crane lift a junk car from one place and then drop the car in a different place. What **hypothesis** could Rocco form about what was on the end of the crane to move the car?

   There was an electromagnet on the end of the crane.

18. Paul found a bag of coins in a closet. None of the coins was attracted by a magnet. What could Paul **infer** about the coins?

   The coins were not attracted to a magnet because they did not contain iron.

Name _____

Critical Thinking 10 points each

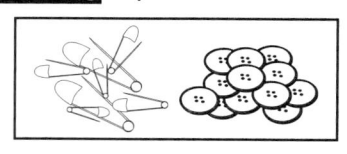

19. Bailey found a mixture of plastic buttons and metal safety pins in her grandmother's sewing box. She wanted to separate the buttons and the pins. What hypothesis could Bailey form about a method to quickly separate the pins from the buttons?

   Possible answer: The pins could be quickly pulled out by using a magnet to attract them.

20. Debbie found some magnets, but the ends of the magnets were not all marked north or south. She experimented with two of the magnets, and the results are shown in the drawing.

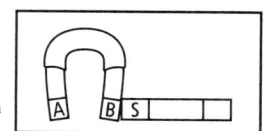

   Identify the poles of the horseshoe magnet. Explain how you know.

   Possible answer: End B is north because it is attracted to the south pole of the bar magnet, and opposite poles attract. End A must be south.

Unit E • Chapter 14

Name _____
Date _____

Chapter Assessment

Heat, Light, and Sound

Vocabulary 4 points each

Use the terms from the box to complete the sentences.

| absorbed | conductor | insulator | opaque |
| reflection | pitch | thermal energy | shadow |

1. When light strikes an object, some of it is taken in, or __**absorbed**__

2. Objects that block light are __**opaque**__

3. A dark area that forms when an object blocks the path of light is called a __**shadow**__

4. The movement of heat between objects with different temperatures is __**thermal energy**__

5. An object that doesn't conduct heat well is called an __**insulator**__

6. How high or low a sound is is called __**pitch**__

7. An object that heat can move through easily is called a __**conductor**__

8. The bouncing of light off an object is called __**reflection**__

Name _____

Science Concepts 4 points each

Write the letter of the best choice.

__B__ 9. Which of the following is a good conductor?
   A. cloth   C. plastic
   B. copper   D. wood

__G__ 10. Which of the following is a good insulator?
   F. aluminum   H. iron
   G. cloth   J. silver

__A__ 11. When can you see a reflection in a surface?
   A. when the surface is smooth and shiny
   B. when the surface is rough and uneven
   C. when the surface is black
   D. You can never see a reflection.

__J__ 12. What do you call a dark area that forms when an object blocks the path of light?
   F. a block   H. refraction
   G. a rainbow   J. a shadow

__C__ 13. When light hits an object, some of the light is reflected. What happens to the light that is not reflected?
   A. It is translucent.   C. It is absorbed.
   B. It turns white.   D. It retracts.

__G__ 14. Which of the following is translucent?
   F. desk   H. mirror
   G. light bulb   J. rocks

__C__ 15. When you talk about a sound's pitch, to what are you referring?
   A. how long or short the sound is
   B. how loud or soft the sound is
   C. how high or low the sound is
   D. the speed at which the sound travels

Name _____

__H__ 16. Which of these does **not** produce vibrations?
   F. plucking strings on a harp
   G. blowing on a flute
   H. lifting a trumpet
   J. tapping on a drum

Inquiry Skills 8 points each

17. Jamie went outside on a cloudy day. She hoped to see a rainbow. The sun was not out, and it had just finished raining. **Predict** whether she will see a rainbow. Explain.

   Possible answer: Rainbows are visible only on days when the sun is out and there are water droplets in the air. Even though there are rain droplets on this day, there will not be a rainbow because there are no rays of sunlight to pass through the raindrops.

18. You are wearing a shirt that reads "TOMATO" and you stand in front of a mirror. **Infer** what you will see in the mirror.

   Possible answer: Since the reflection in a mirror is reversed from left to right, the word will read "OTAMOT." (Since all of the letters in *TOMATO* are symmetrical, the letters themselves won't be reversed.)

Name _____

Critical Thinking 10 points each

19. Jenna is wearing a down jacket. The jacket has many air spaces. Will the jacket keep Jenna warm? Explain.

   Possible answer: The jacket will keep Jenna warm because air is an insulator. The air keeps the heat from moving away from the body.

20. Look at the picture of the boats. Both people will hear the motorboat passing, but who will hear the sound more loudly? Why?

   Possible answer: The person snorkeling underwater will hear the sound more loudly because sound moves farther and faster through liquids than it does through air.

Answer Key

Unit E

Unit Assessment

Write the letter of the best choice. **4 points each**

B 1. Which property of sound shows how much energy it has?
   A. eardrum
   B. loudness
   C. pitch
   D. vibration

F 2. Which action causes a chemical change?
   F. burning paper
   G. tearing paper
   H. drawing with a crayon on paper
   J. crumpling paper

B 3. What does this picture show?
   A. absorption
   B. reflection
   C. refraction
   D. shadow

G 4. Which kind of object stops thermal energy from moving between objects?
   F. conductor
   G. insulator
   H. metal
   J. thermometer

B 5. Which resource is a fossil fuel?
   A. electricity
   B. oil
   C. sunlight
   D. water

J 6. Which of these classroom objects will a magnet most likely pick up?
   F. rubber eraser
   G. plastic cup
   H. chalk
   J. metal paper clip

A 7. What does an electromagnet use to turn a piece of metal into a magnet?
   A. electric current
   B. iron
   C. lightning
   D. wind

H 8. What do mass, volume, and density have in common?
   F. They tell how much matter is in an object.
   G. They tell how much space an object takes up.
   H. They are physical properties of matter.
   J. They cannot be measured.

D 9. Water boils at 100°C. Chocolate melts at about 35°C. What can you conclude from these facts?
   A. There is no relationship between temperature and heat energy.
   B. It takes the same amount of heat energy to melt chocolate as it does to boil water.
   C. It takes more heat energy to melt chocolate than to boil water.
   D. It takes more heat energy to boil water than to melt chocolate.

H 10. How does light travel?
   F. in circles
   G. in curves
   H. in straight lines
   J. in a zigzag pattern

B 11. How will the poles of these magnets react as they move closer together?
   A. They will attract.
   B. They will repel.
   C. There will be no reaction.
   D. The magnets will stick together.

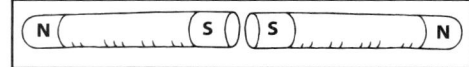

F 12. Which material most easily conducts current electricity?
   F. copper
   G. plastic
   H. rubber
   J. wood

C 13. A ball is sitting at the top of a hill. It rolls down the hill and then stops at the bottom. When does the ball have kinetic energy?
   A. before it rolls down the hill
   B. before and after it rolls down the hill
   C. as it is rolling down the hill
   D. never

J 14. Which observation best demonstrates that gasoline provides energy?
   F. Gasoline can burn.
   G. Gasoline is a fossil fuel.
   H. Gasoline evaporates.
   J. Gasoline can make a car move.

A 15. Gene uses a tank of helium to fill balloons for a party. He observes that the helium will fill a balloon of any shape or size. In which state of matter is the helium?
   A. gas
   B. liquid
   C. solid
   D. all of the above

F 16. What kind of energy turns on the light bulb in this circuit?
   F. current electricity
   G. kinetic energy
   H. solar energy
   J. static electricity

A 17. What happens to drinking water if enough heat is added to it?
   A. It changes from a liquid to a gas.
   B. It changes from a liquid to a solid.
   C. It changes from a solid to a liquid.
   D. It changes from a gas to a liquid.

Unit E / Unit F • Chapter 15

Name _____

__J__ 18. Which of the following is a solution?
 F. sand and rocks
 G. sand and water
 H. raisins baked in bread
 J. salt and water

__C__ 19. What color or colors does a red T-shirt absorb?
 A. red only
 B. blue and green
 C. all colors but red
 D. all colors

Write the answer to each question. 6 points each

20. Explain how you know that air is matter.
 Possible answer: Air takes up space. It fills balloons, lungs, and the atmosphere. Even though you cannot see air, you know it is there. You can see it move other things, and you can feel it on your skin.

21. Compare and contrast renewable and nonrenewable resources. How are they alike? How are they different? Give examples of each kind of resource in your answer.
 Possible answer: Renewable and nonrenewable resources are both resources, or things from nature that people can use. Fossil fuels, for example, are a resource that people use for energy. Renewable resources, such as solar energy, can be replaced during a human lifetime. Nonrenewable resources, such as oil and coal, cannot.

Unit E (page 5 of 6) Assessment Guide AG 113

Name _____

22. Lightning is an example of static electricity. Explain why.
 Possible answer: Static electricity is an electric charge that builds up in an object. Lightning occurs when electric charge builds up in a cloud and moves to the ground in a flash of light.

23. Describe the conditions needed for a rainbow to form. Explain how a rainbow forms.
 Possible answer: The conditions needed for a rainbow to form are sunlight and water droplets in the air. The water droplets act like prisms. They separate the sunlight (white light) into its many colors.

AG 114 Assessment Guide (page 6 of 6) Unit E

Name _____
Date _____

Chapter Assessment

Forces and Motion

Vocabulary 4 points each

Match each term in Column B with its meaning in Column A.

Column A	Column B
__D__ 1. Force that pulls two objects toward each other	A. distance
__H__ 2. Change of position	B. trough
__E__ 3. Disturbance that travels through matter or space	C. force
__A__ 4. How far it is from one place to another	D. gravity
__G__ 5. Highest point of a wave	E. wave
__B__ 6. Lowest part of a wave	F. speed
__F__ 7. Distance an object moves in a certain period of time	G. crest
__C__ 8. Any kind of push or pull	H. motion

Science Concepts 4 points each

Write the letter of the best choice.

__A__ 9. What does a ruler measure?
 A. distance C. speed
 B. motion D. weight

__G__ 10. Which surface would cause the **least** friction?
 F. dirt H. grass
 G. ice J. rocks

Unit F • Chapter 15 (page 1 of 4) Assessment Guide AG 115

Name _____

__B__ 11. The strength of a force and the direction of a force affect the motion of an object. What is the third thing that affects the object's motion?
 A. color C. texture
 B. mass D. volume

__H__ 12. Which object would be **most** affected by magnetic force?
 F. a marble H. a paper clip
 G. a pillow J. a wooden fence

__C__ 13. Which object would take the **least** amount of force to move?
 A. a book C. a pencil
 B. a car D. a table

__H__ 14. Look at the picture. What part of the wave is the arrow pointing to?
 F. crest
 G. disturbance
 H. trough
 J. wavelength

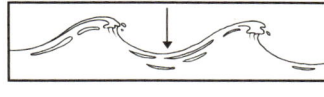

__B__ 15. There is a book on the table. You push the book to the left. At the same time, your friend pushes the book to the right. What is the net force on the book?
 A. your friend's push
 B. your push plus your friend's push
 C. your push
 D. the weight of the book

__H__ 16. How do scientists figure out the speed of a wave?
 F. by measuring its height
 G. by measuring its depth
 H. by measuring its wavelength
 J. by measuring the water's temperature

AG 116 Assessment Guide (page 2 of 4) Unit F • Chapter 15

Answer Key (page 23 of 26) Assessment Guide AG 155

Unit F • Chapter 15/Chapter 16

Name _____

Inquiry Skills 8 points each

17. Look at the data below. **Interpret the data** to determine how far Runner 1 ran and how long it took her. Which runner ran the farthest?

	Distance	Direction	Time
Runner 1	1 mile	Northeast	7 min 10 sec
Runner 2	1.5 miles	South	9 min 23 sec
Runner 3	2 miles	Southwest	15 min 14 sec

Runner 1 ran 1 mile in 7 minutes and 10 seconds. Runner 3 ran the farthest.

18. Michael is going to conduct an investigation to **compare** the speed of a turtle with the speed of a rabbit. What should he use to measure their speeds? How should he conduct the investigation?

Possible answer: Michael could use a stopwatch to measure time and a meterstick to measure distance. Speed is the measure of an object's change in position during a unit of time, so in the investigation, he would have to measure both distance and time.

Unit F • Chapter 15   (page 3 of 4)   Assessment Guide   AG 117

Name _____

Critical Thinking 10 points each

19. If friction did not exist, could you ride a bicycle? Why or why not?

No. Without friction, the tires would just slide around and you couldn't get the bike to move forward. Also, the brakes would not work.

20. Jeremy and his friend are playing basketball. Describe two forces that are involved when Jeremy shoots a basketball through the net.

Possible answers (any two): Shooting is a push. Gravity pulls the ball through the net. Friction between his shoes and the floor allows Jeremy to stand still while shooting.

AG 118   Assessment Guide   (page 4 of 4)   Unit F • Chapter 15

Name _____
Date _____

Chapter Assessment

Work and Machines

Vocabulary 4 points each

Match each term in Column B with its meaning in Column A.

Column A

G 1. Two inclined planes placed back to back
D 2. A wheel with a rope around it
A 3. The fixed point on a lever
E 4. A simple machine that is like a nail with threads wrapped around it
H 5. Using force to move an object
B 6. A simple machine that makes moving and lifting things easier
C 7. A bar that turns on a fixed point
F 8. A machine that needs only one force to make it work

Column B
A. fulcrum
B. inclined plane
C. lever
D. pulley
E. screw
F. simple machine
G. wedge
H. work

Science Concepts 4 points each

Write the letter of the best choice.

D 9. What type of simple machine is a screwdriver?
A. inclined plane   C. pulley
B. lever   D. wheel-and-axle

F 10. Tasha is making a poster to show pictures of levers. Which object should **not** be on her poster?
F. nail   H. broom
G. rake   J. crowbar

Unit F • Chapter 16   (page 1 of 4)   Assessment Guide   AG 121

Name _____

D 11. How is the shovel being used in this picture?
A. as a wheel-and-axle
B. as a wedge
C. as an inclined plane
D. as a lever

F 12. A screw is made of a post and another kind of simple machine. What is that other kind of simple machine?
F. inclined plane   H. wedge
G. pulley   J. wheel-and-axle

B 13. Levon's class is learning about simple machines. His teacher has written the names of four simple machines in a table on the board. As she points to each name, Levon gives an example of that machine. She writes down what he says. Which simple machine is correctly paired with its example?
A. lever
B. wedge
C. pulley
D. inclined plane

Simple Machine	Example
lever	wheelchair ramp
wedge	knife
pulley	screwdriver
inclined plane	seesaw

H 14. A jar lid has threads. These threads help hold the lid tightly on the jar. What simple machine is a jar lid?
F. lever   H. screw
G. pulley   J. wedge

AG 122   Assessment Guide   (page 2 of 4)   Unit F • Chapter 16

AG 156   Assessment Guide   (page 24 of 26)   **Answer Key**

Unit F • Chapter 16/Unit F

Name _____

__D__ 15. Which of these is **not** an example of work?
  A. lifting a book   C. drawing with a marker
  B. opening a door   D. adding numbers in your head

__F__ 16. Mr. Lopez is telling his class about the human body. He describes how some athletes lift weights to make their arms stronger. An athlete holds a weight in her hand and bends her arm at the elbow. The elbow acts as a fulcrum.
  In his example, the arm is a simple machine. Which machine is it?
  F. lever
  G. pulley
  H. screw
  J. wheel-and-axle

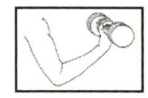

Inquiry Skills 8 points each

17. Megan needs to keep a door propped open. **Predict** which simple machine Megan will choose to do the job. Explain.

  Megan will choose a wedge. She will push the wedge between the door and the floor. The wedge will keep the door open.

18. **Interpret** the pictures to decide which screw is easier to turn. Explain.

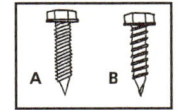

  Screw A is easier to turn, because it has threads that are closer together.

Unit F • Chapter 16   (page 3 of 4)   Assessment Guide   AG 123

Name _____

Critical Thinking 10 points each

19. The pictures show two simple machines. Tell how the machines are alike.

  Possible answer: Both are simple machines that can be used to raise an object. When a person pulls down on one end of the pulley rope, the other end—with the bucket—moves upward. In the same way, when a person pushes down on one end of the lever, the other end—with the bucket—moves upward.

20. Luis has made two ramps. Ramp A is steeper than Ramp B. Which ramp will make it easier for Luis to move the block of wood? Tell how you know.

  Possible answer: Ramp B will be easier, because it is less steep. This means that Luis will use less force to push the block of wood up Ramp B than up Ramp A.

AG 124   Assessment Guide   (page 4 of 4)   Unit F • Chapter 16

Name _____
Date _____

Unit Assessment

Write the letter of the best choice. 4 points each

__B__ 1. Two tug-of-war teams are pulling in opposite directions on a rope. The rope does not move. Why?
  A. There are no forces acting on the rope.
  B. The net force is zero.
  C. The rope has too much mass.
  D. Gravity is too strong.

__H__ 2. Which of the following is a simple machine?
  F. pillow   H. broom
  G. dishwasher   J. engine

__C__ 3. Why does it take less force to turn a screw into wood than to drive a nail into wood?
  A. Screws are shorter than nails.
  B. Screws act like levers, so they apply a greater force than nails.
  C. The threads on the screw increase the distance it travels.
  D. Screws do more work than nails.

__F__ 4. Which wave has the longest wavelength?

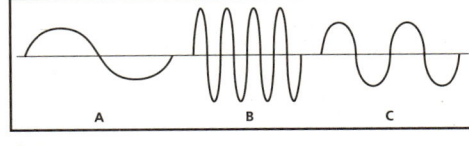

  F. Wave A
  G. Wave B
  H. Wave C
  J. There is not enough information to decide.

Unit F   (page 1 of 6)   Assessment Guide   AG 127

Name _____

__D__ 5. Why does the same force move a baseball farther than a bowling ball?
  A. The baseball is softer.
  B. The baseball has a rougher surface.
  C. The baseball has less volume.
  D. The baseball has less mass.

__F__ 6. What type of simple machine is a seesaw?

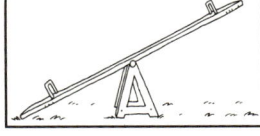

  F. lever
  G. pulley
  H. wheel-and-axle
  J. all of the above

__B__ 7. A dog pushes a bone across the floor. The bone moves to the left. In which direction did the dog probably push the bone?
  A. right
  B. left
  C. down
  D. up

__J__ 8. Which two measurements are needed to find the speed of an object?
  F. force and mass
  G. time and wavelength
  H. position and force
  J. time and distance

AG 128   Assessment Guide   (page 2 of 6)   Unit F

Answer Key   (page 25 of 26)   **Assessment Guide**   AG 157

Unit F

Name _____

A 9. Which simple machine would best help movers put boxes in the back of a tall truck?
   A. inclined plane
   B. screw
   C. wedge
   D. wheel-and-axle

G 10. Which activity would a scientist say involves work?
   F. watching a movie
   G. opening a door
   H. leaning against a wall
   J. thinking about homework

D 11. What is the main purpose of a wedge?

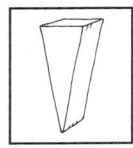

   A. to raise an object
   B. to change the direction of an object
   C. to speed up an object
   D. to split an object apart

H 12. Why are waves able to move matter?
   F. They have speed.
   G. They have long wavelengths.
   H. They carry energy.
   J. They have weight.

Name _____

C 13. What type of simple machine could best be used to close curtains?
   A. inclined plane
   B. lever
   C. pulley
   D. wheel-and-axle

F 14. Which statement about force is **false**?
   F. Forces always start objects moving.
   G. A moving object will keep moving until a force stops it.
   H. The stronger the force, the greater the change in motion.
   J. An object moves in the direction of the force pushing or pulling it.

B 15. What is the main purpose of a machine?
   A. to change the speed of an object
   B. to change the way work is done
   C. to turn an object
   D. to eliminate work

J 16. Tyrese pulls a chair across the floor. Which two things would he need to measure to find the amount of work he has done?
   F. distance and time
   G. time and wavelength
   H. time and force
   J. force and distance

B 17. Which force always pulls objects toward Earth?
   A. friction
   B. gravity
   C. magnetic force
   D. net force

Name _____

J 18. What type of simple machine is a doorknob?

   F. lever   H. screw
   G. pulley   J. wheel-and-axle

A 19. Two airplanes, A and B, leave an airport at the same time. They each fly for 2 hours. Airplane A travels 800 miles. Airplane B travels 600 miles. How is this possible?
   A. Airplane A flew at a greater speed.
   B. Airplane B flew at a greater speed.
   C. Airplane A flew a shorter distance.
   D. Airplane B flew a longer time.

Write the answer to each question. 6 points each

20. Suppose your job is to lift a heavy box onto a platform. Describe two different ways you could use a simple machine to move the box. Explain how each machine changes the way you do work.

   Possible answer: I could push the box up a ramp. A ramp increases the distance the box moves, but it decreases the force needed to move it. I could also use a pulley. A pulley makes work easier because you pull down on a rope rather than lift up a box.

Name _____

21. Suppose you are playing soccer. Identify two things that affect how far you kick the ball. Describe the effects of each one.

   Possible answer: The motion of an object is affected by its mass and the amount of force applied to it. The greater the force (how hard you kick the ball), the farther the ball will go. If the ball had a different mass, the same amount of force would move it a different distance.

22. Summarize the relationship between speed, distance, and time. Use speed to explain how two cars can leave at the same time and travel the same route but arrive at different times.

   Possible answer: Speed is the distance an object moves in a certain amount of time. Speed relates distance to time. The two cars that go the same distance in different times travel at different speeds.

23. Tara pushes very hard on a box of books. No matter how hard she pushes, the box does not move. Does Tara do work? Explain.

   Possible answer: Tara does not do work. She applies a force, but the object does not move. According to scientists, work is done only when a force moves an object. If the object does not move, no work is done.

Curr
Q161.2
.H77
2009
Gr.3
Assess. Guide

DISCARDED
MILLSTEIN LIBRARY

MILLSTEIN LIBRARY
UNIVERSITY OF PITTSBURGH
AT GREENSBURG